Vitasta Publishing acknowledges and asserts the copyright of Avtar Mota, The Parimu Family and Kapil Kaul (artist) (Pages xii, 47 top, 48) for the pictures that appear in the book. The cover painting featured is photographed by John Alvord.

landscape & lament

Art, Exile and the Rebel Artist

landscape & lament

Art, Exile and the Rebel Artist

AVTAR MOTA

Vitasta

Published by
Vitasta Publishing Pvt Ltd
2/15, Ansari Road, Daryaganj
New Delhi - 110 002
info@vitastapublishing.com

ISBN 978-93-90961-77-1

First Edition 2023

MRP ₹ 995

VITASTA TEAM: Renu Kaul Verma, Papri Sri Raman, Somesh Kumar Mishra
Printed by Saurabh Printers Pvt. Ltd.

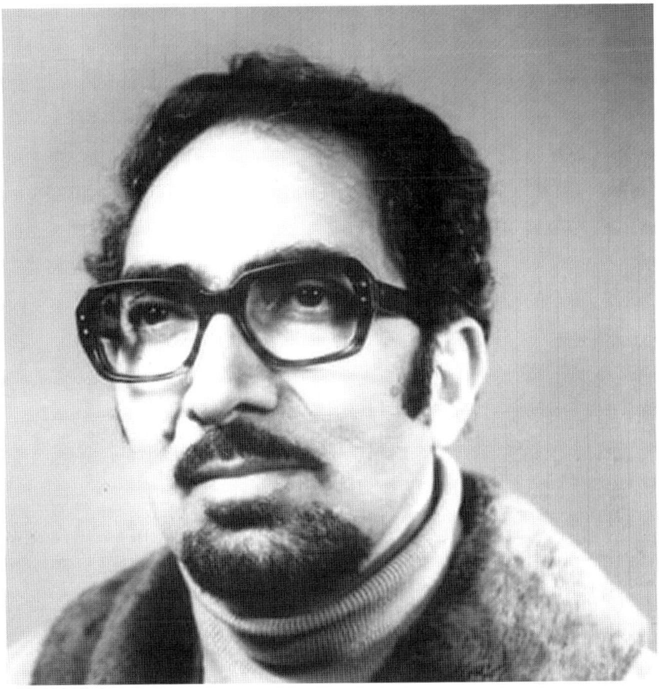

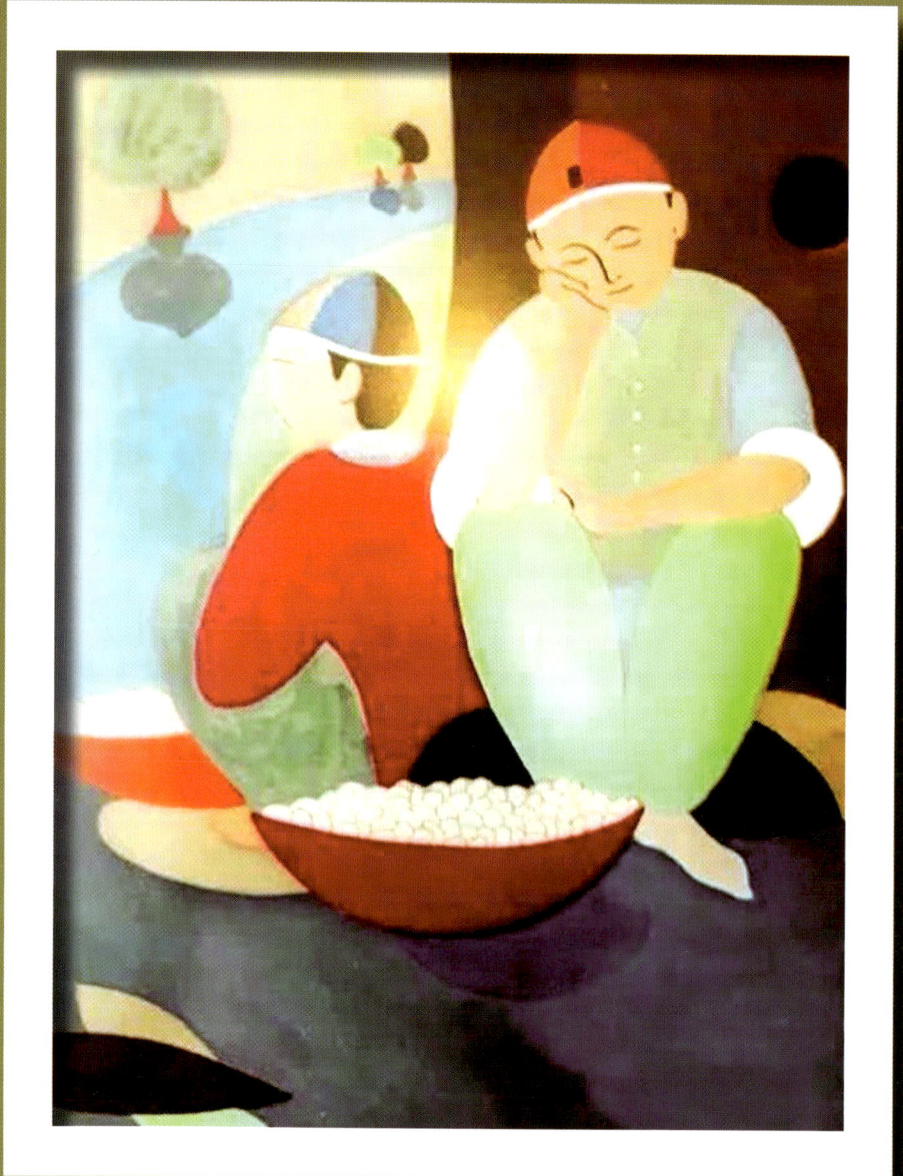

The Eggseller 1950

for

Impa Agarwal Mota,
Jeanne Allard Mota,
Aanya Mota and Siya Mota

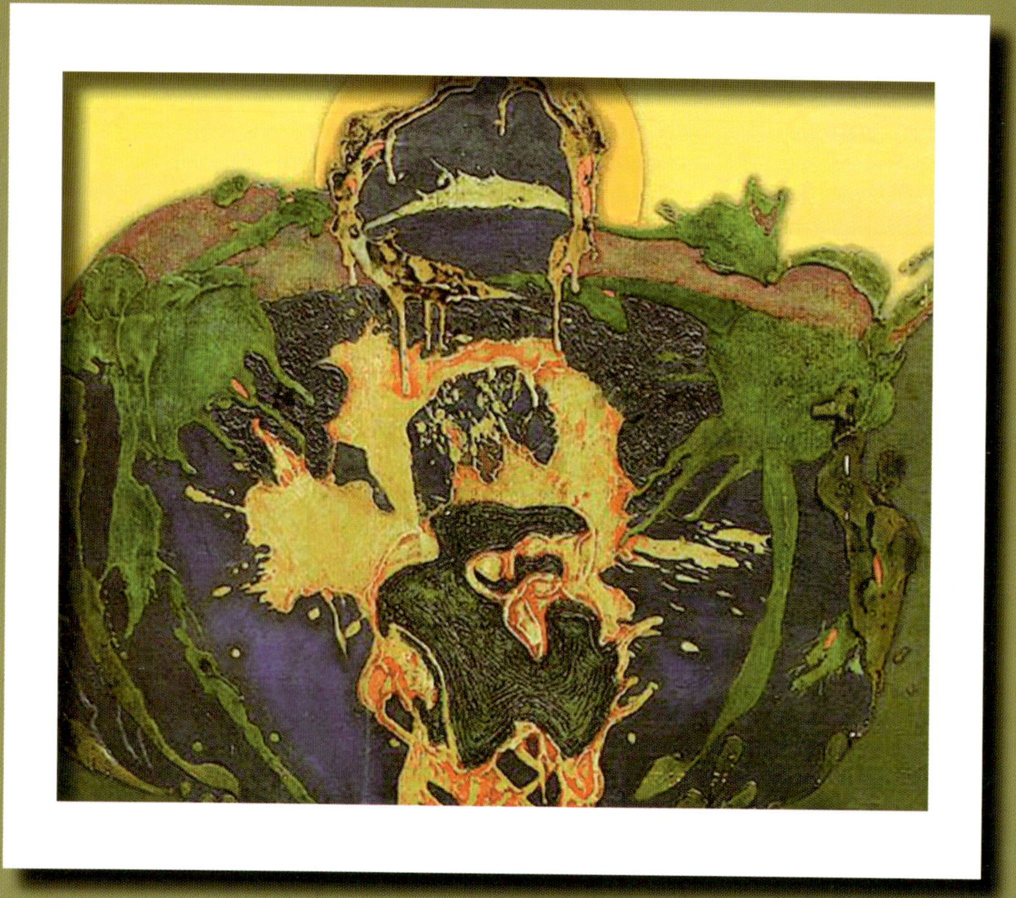

Parimu Abstract

TABLE OF **CONTENTS**

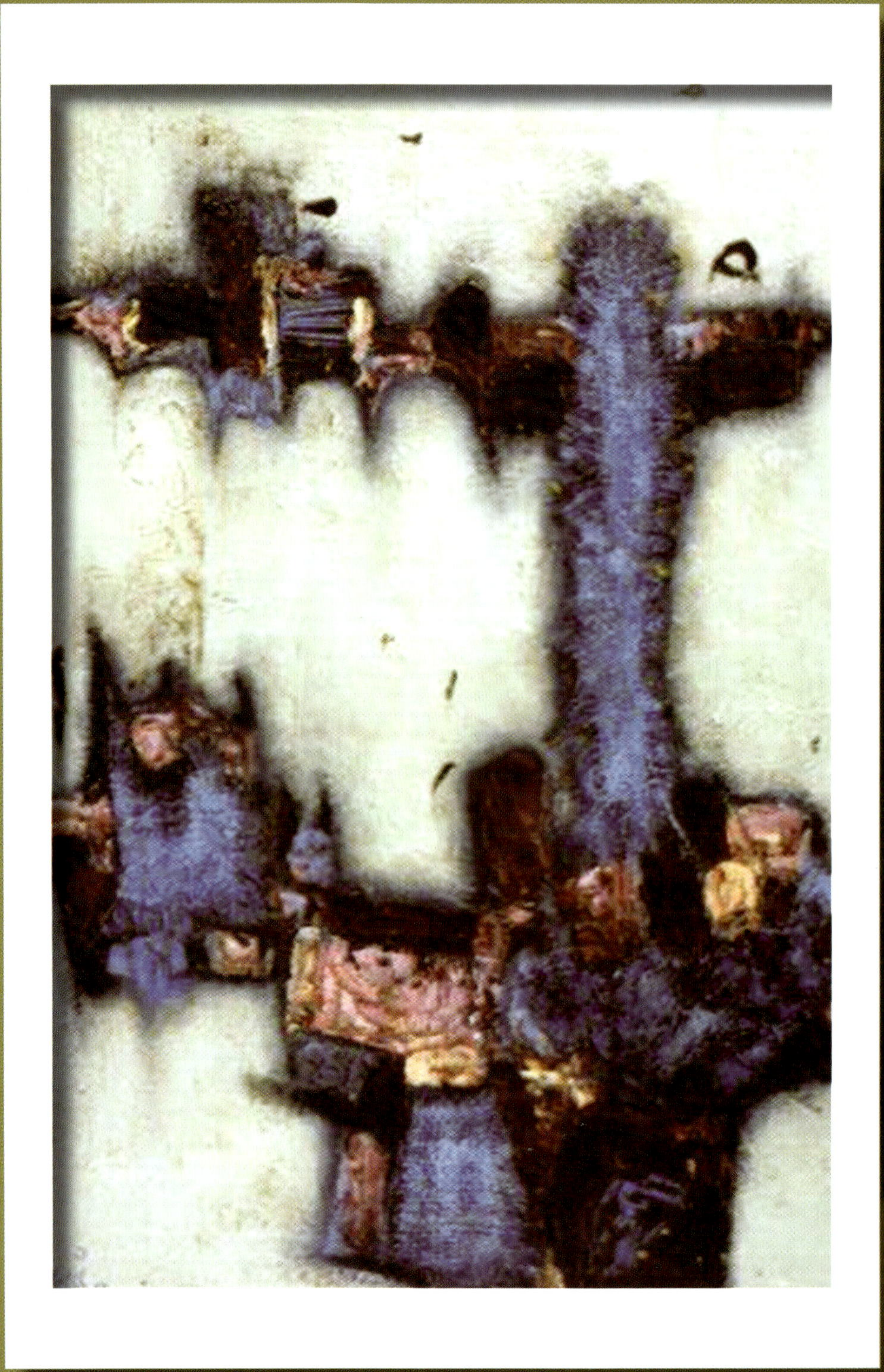

Parimu Abstract

If all the world were clear, art would not exist
—Albert Camus

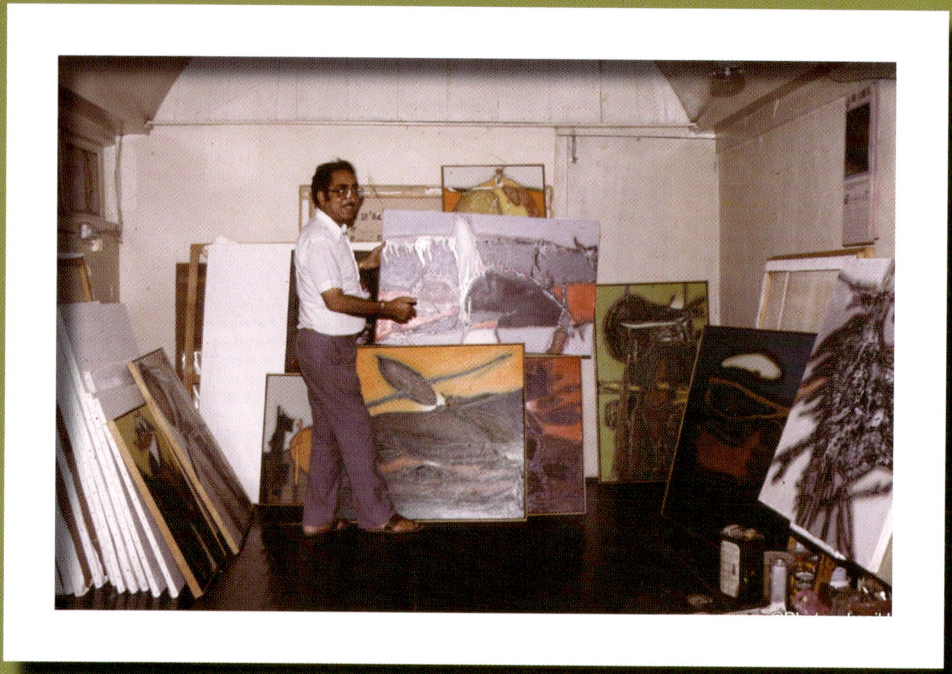

Bansi Parimu in his Studio, Takhleeq

PREFACE

Art washes away from the soul the dust of everyday life
—Pablo Picasso

Since 1982, I have been visiting various museums and art galleries. Many photographs were clicked, and many details were regularly recorded by me without any mission or immediate purpose. Many friends kept on provoking me to give all this record a proper shape and some place for posterity. My hectic bank job prevented me from attending to this work. After superannuation, sometime around 2016, I set out on a serious mission to do what I could not do while in banking. I decided to write a book on the journey of Kashmir's art and the unsung artist, Bansi Parimu.

Bansi Parimu's work and personality had fascinated me from my college days. To me, he was an embodiment of struggle. The struggle of a man from starvation to settlement. Settlement on the basis of sheer merit and hard work. Even when he never entered college to procure a degree, he proved a far better human being than many of his degree-holding contemporaries. He learned the art by total observation and self-education by putting into practice the philosophy of neither this nor that, i.e. the significance of the view is in the eye of the beholder; that which in our philosophy is known as *neti, neti*. All this appealed to me as something rare.

The task of compiling this book had many difficulties.

This project was solely dependent on external sources. After 1990, everything had changed its location and setting. Many people needed to be interviewed at scattered places. Many things needed to be looked into from several sources. Parimu had emerged from the rich artistic traditions of Kashmir. The linkages had to be traced from many sources to one proper perspective. That was really a challenging task. Help came from unexpected quarters. Possibly within their heart, every person wanted to see documented his or her tribute to a man who was selfless, self-made and full of humanism and compassion. I pooled in my own notes, photographs and details that had been collected over the years from visits to many art galleries and museums, both within the country and outside with resources from some others to put this volume together. While documenting the journey of the unsung artist Bansi Parimu, this book also narrates the journey of art in Kashmir from Burzohama stone drawings to the modern period and the many traumas artists and their artistic endeavours faced through the millennium.

Help came primarily from the immediate family of Bansi Parimu. I thank them profusely, especially Jaya Parimu, wife of the artist, who herself is a connoisseur of music and art. She taught music at various degree colleges in the State. My thanks are due to all the respondents who find mention in the book. I thank Dr Kashi Nath Pandita (historian, author and Persian scholar) for his regular guidance, Ashok Ogra (media personality, educator, writer, and former head, Discovery Channel, South Asia) for his suggestions, Tsering Tashi (Deputy Director, Department of Archives, Archeology and Museums J&K government, Jammu) for providing access to the department's library and old archival records, Anish Sharma, the young assistant in the library of Archives who was always helpful in providing the desired books and sought after reference materials, Narinder Safaya, advocate Supreme Court of India for arranging some photographs, I K Kilam for reading the manuscript and Arvind Gigoo for giving my manuscript the shape of a book.

I remain grateful to the staff of Dogra Art Gallery, Jammu for all the help they extended during my visits. I remain indebted to many friends, acquaintances, families, learned authors, photographers, and writers whose books and photographs find mention in my work. I have tried to name each and every source, and still, if I have missed something, that remains an inadvertent omission.

I also need to thank my immediate family for being supportive and encouraging me to complete the manuscript. My thanks to many friends in the Kashmir valley who have volunteered help in this project and who were always telling me, 'why don't you write a book?' and to whom, I would always convey my sincere feelings through the following couplets of Urdu poet Amjad Islam Amjad. I quote:

Bhatke huve phirte hain kayee lafz jo dil mein
Duniyaa ne diyaa waqt to likheinge kissi din
Khushboo ki tarah misl e saba khaak numaa se
Galiyon se teri shehar ki guzareinge kissi din.

So many vagrant words keep tossing in my mind,
Should this world grant me some moments,
Then, surely, I shall write them down.
Like the fragrance of morning breeze,
One day I shall flit past through
the dust of your city's lanes.

Further, during the time the manuscript was completed, and it got published, the State of Jammu and Kashmir was bifurcated into two Union Territories: Ladakh and J&K. It was not possible for me to change the manuscript at many places at that stage. Accordingly, 'J&K State' wherever mentioned by me needs to be understood and read in the light of these changes.

Avtar Mota
akm24776@gmail.com

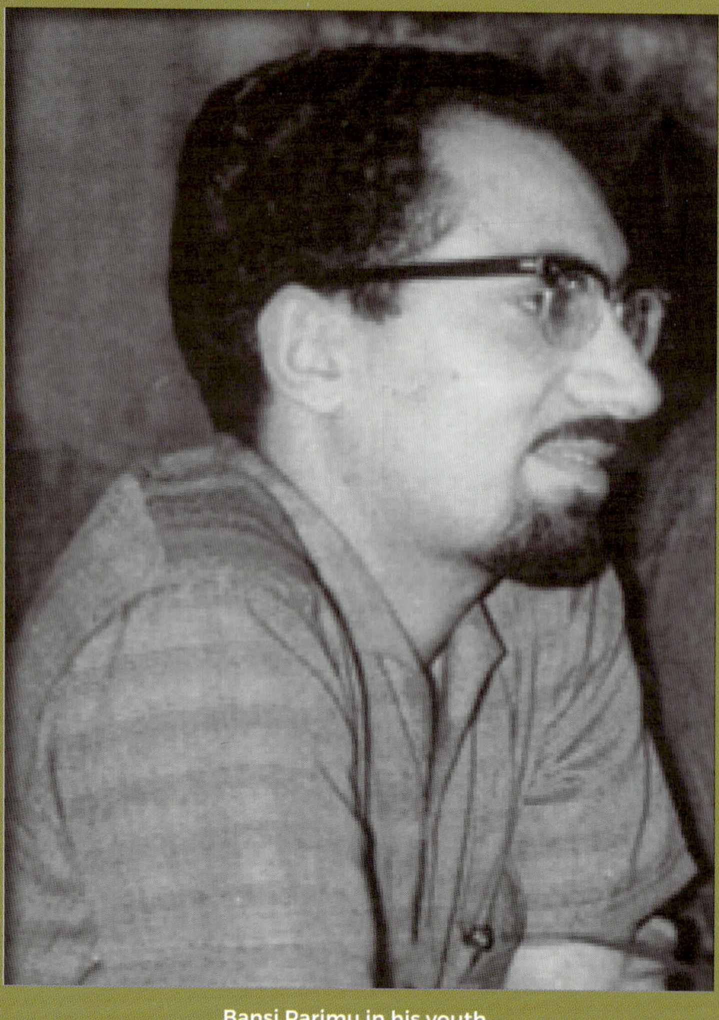

Bansi Parimu in his youth

THE REBEL

THE ART MOST eloquently describes the artist and his rebellion. The Kashmiri artist Bansi Parimu's work places him firmly among the versatile twentieth century artists from India whose brush spoke for the people, whose colours painted rebellion and sorrow, whose canvas stretched beyond imagination. Known as a rebel artist, no doubt Parimu was a modernist but not a typical modernist, his art leapt from medium to medium defying the limits of convention. Thus, he was not only non-conformist, but he was also curious and creative as an artist. His art was definitely angry, and his palette represented the griefs of the common people.

M F Husain said about Parimu, 'A dedicated painter from Kashmir whom I came to know from my early sixty (1960-1965) visits. We became friends. His work gained stature that could reflect the beauty and turmoil of the Kashmiri people. The colour, the sound of its landscape creates an orchestra of nature's bounty. Parimu's paintings keep singing the song of creation that is Kashmir on our planet'.

Describing his artistic journey, a website devoted to Parimu's art says:

> He had a distinctive and individualistic style of 'Abstract Landscapes' which earned him a special place in the world of contemporary Indian art. He had come a long way from the earlier realistic watercolours that had once thrilled him. More organic than geometrical, the modern abstractionism of his

369 dadabhai naoroji road, bombay 400 001
telephone: (022) 284 1837 telefax: (099) 904 8473

PUNDOLE ART GALLERY

A dedicated painter from Kashmir whom I came to know during my early sixty visits. We became friends and his works gained a stature that could reflect the beauty and turmoil of Kashmiri people. The colour, the sound of its landscape create an orchestra of nature's bounty.

Parimu's painting keep singing the song of creation that is Kashmir on our planet.

Husain
1 jan. 2001

work was marked by his strong association with the valley, which remained the inspiration of his creativity right up to his death. Particularly enchanting was his use of fine gauze overlays, calligraphic and arabesque at a time, which seemed to capture the changing pattern of light in the Himalayan pastures.

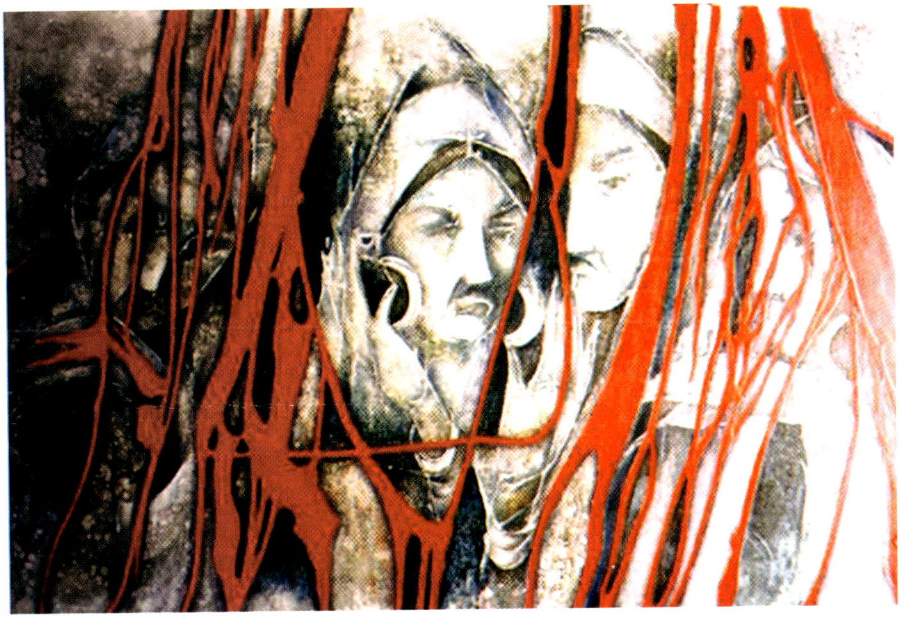

Red Knows No Creed

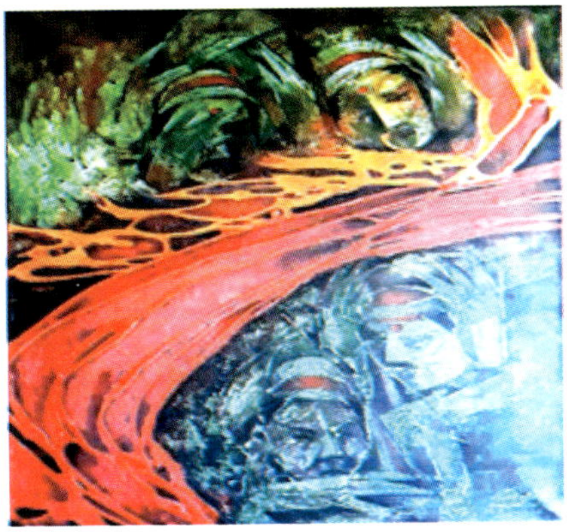

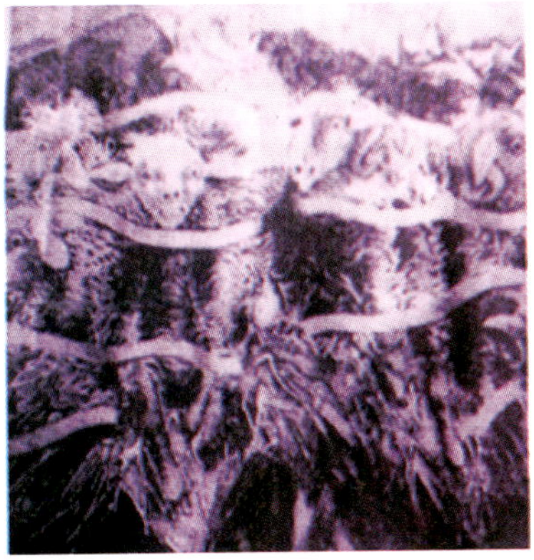

The Red Divide 1990 (Left); Charging Rams, a photo from a newspaper clipping

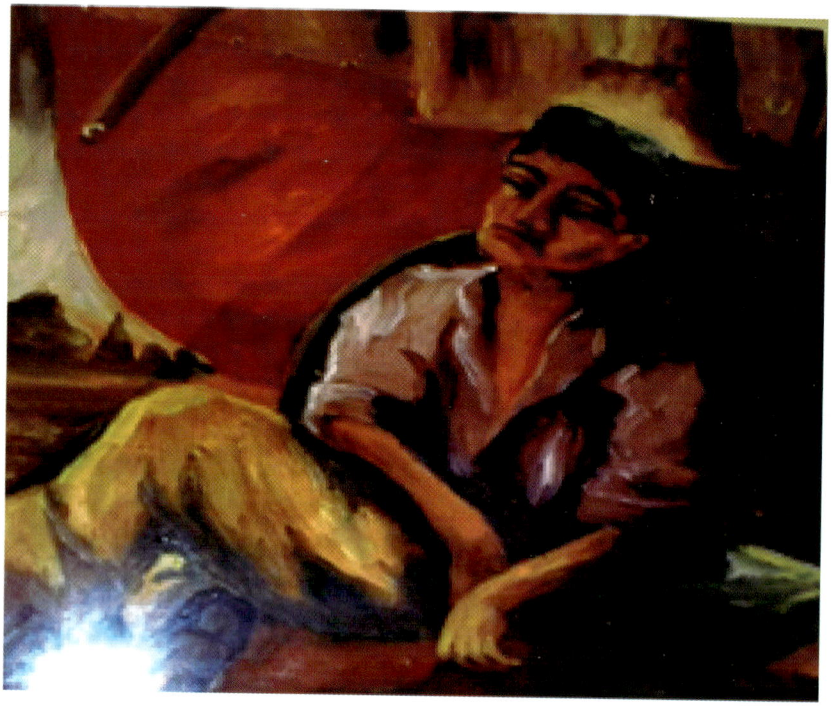

A Rickshaw puller taking a nap

Bansi Parimu was a nonconformist from his childhood. He would jump into unknown and unfamiliar waters, and always swim against the current without bothering about the consequences. In his childhood, the rebel in him did something unexpected. One day, not finding his father around, young Bansi threw all the idols of the deities in his father's Pooja room into the waters of the Jhelum River nearby. A good thrashing from his father left a wound on his head and the scar remained there lifelong.

His was the loudest voice against any communalism or divisive politics. The attacks on the temples and houses of Kashmiri Pandits engineered by some politicians from Anantnaag in February 1986 pained him. It was something he could not reconcile with. It was a challenge to his lifelong beliefs and convictions. H K Dua published a story about these attacks in *The Indian Express* of 3 March 1986, writing:

> The minority community of the Kashmiri Pandits has suffered discrimination under successive regimes in the Valley but the Anantnaag communal riots have left them in a state of shock. The recent violence has shattered their confidence. They are feeling bitter, frustrated, and bewildered. The attacks on houses, places of worship on 20 February, particularly in places like Wanpoh, Dhanav, Bongund and Lukbhawan in Ananatnaag district and incidents in Srinagar, Sopore, and Baramulla involving the beating and harassment of members of the minority community have further intensified their anxiety and generated a feeling of insecurity.

Parimu blamed politicians in the State for engineering the attacks to gain political mileage. To his friends, he said, 'This is something for which all of us should feel ashamed. We have one mother tongue, common culture, and history of centuries-old common suffering. Some leaders are hell-bent upon creating a wedge. We must stand up and fight it jointly'.

In the interview that he gave to Shams ul Islam for the 4 August 1991 issue of *The Times of India* under the title, 'Donkeys Grazing on a Saffron Field', he was biting in his criticism:

> Kashmir's present tragedy is the living example of what petty politicians can do to people with a glorious history of peace and brotherhood. The rulers in Delhi and their henchmen in the Valley systematically aimed at undermining the values, life norms and culture of the Kashmiris.

When the J&K State Academy of Art, Culture, and Languages wanted to award him in the 1970s – to be presented to him by the then chief minister in a public function – not only did he turn down the award, he went on to deride the chief minister for ignoring the plight of Kashmiri artists. He told the gathering that he could not be silenced by 'crumbs' and asked to compromise with his principles and beliefs. Speaking on his rebel nature, his close friends say:

> For self-respect and dignity, he could kick anything away, the way he tore and threw the government relief cheque into a dustbin. I have with me the cutting of the *Times of India* interview that he gave to Shamsul Islam in August 1991. To Shamsul Islam's question 'why did you refuse to accept the migrant's allowance?' Bansi Parimu replied, 'It is so humiliating. Anyone with self-respect will not seek it'.
>
> —**Agni Shekhar**, Writer and Activist

> He was a rebel who could not be won over with material or any other allurements. I vividly remember how a message once came from Mohammad Shafi Qureshi for Parimu to join the Congress party, but he refused. He was even offered some senior party post and some financial grants, but he declined it all. He was deeply into the politics of Kashmir, with practically no ambition for the chair or money. A real selfless karmyogi.
>
> —**M K Tikoo**, Trustee of Bhagwan Gopinathji Ashram

> He had a strong trait of fearlessness in his personality. It forced him to speak the truth irrespective of personal loss. In 1986, he had an argument with S B Chavan, then minister in the union cabinet. Chavan was in Srinagar in connection with the 'Hangul Conservation Project' started in the J&K State. To the utter surprise of all, Bansi Parimu got up from the audience and spoke directly to the minister about what he felt. He said, 'I believe you are interested in the preservation of the endangered species of the Kashmiri stag or Hangul'. Chavan said, 'It is a project much-sought-after by governor Jagmohan and I too am interested in it.' 'But why can't you do something about the other endangered species here?' asked Bansi Parimu.
>
> 'Which endangered species?', asked Chavan. And pat came the reply from Bansi Parimu, 'Kashmiri Pandits'. This war of words

also finds mention in Anil Maheshwari's book, *Crescent Over Kashmir*, in the chapter, 'Kashmiri Pandits'.

—**Arvind Gigoo**, Author, Poet and Sculptor

He was a man of commitment and conviction. Anything that he found was inappropriate remained so for him, for all times to come. He would not agree to change his opinion even if it meant some loss to him.

—**Makhan Lal Saraf**, Actor, Producer and Playwright

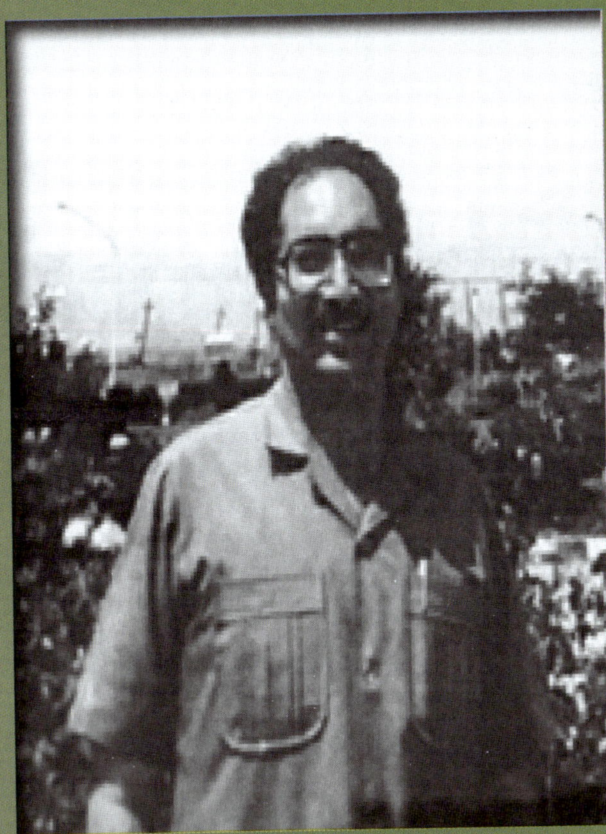

Bansi Parimu in a garden

THE ARTIST AND HIS ART

'SHOCKING' WAS THE word used to describe Edouard Manet's nude masterpiece 'Olympia' (Louvre) when it first appeared in Paris sometime during 1865. Before that, art was meant to be a vehicle for moral and literary commands. After Olympia, art was more obliged to its own devices. As the Naturalist movement in painting developed, the doctrine of 'Art for Art's Sake' became the catchword. 'Modernism' in art emerged in this background of change from the classical. A group of French artists led by Manet, Degas, Monet, Renoir, Pissarro, Sisley, and others stormed the European art scene with their impressionism. This new wave attracted many artists throughout the world. Kashmir could not remain in isolation though it took nearly a century for this wave to cross the Pir Panjal range. D N Walli, S N Butt, Triloke Kaul, and P N Kachru were the first to get influenced by it. Some among this group passed on this new style to all those younger artists who came in their contact. And one of them, Bansi Parimu, was always eager to learn, pick up and practise what any teacher taught him.

Bansi Parimu's work needs to be examined in various phases as it evolved. Parimu's artistic journey has been aptly described by his poet and columnist friend Shantiveer Kaul in 2018:

> Bansi Parimu started from landscapes, experimented with cubism, moved to figurative style and finally settled at pure abstracts. When he painted Kashmir, it always had a deep cultural shade or story to convey. I mean, his paintings like 'Kathi Darwaza' or

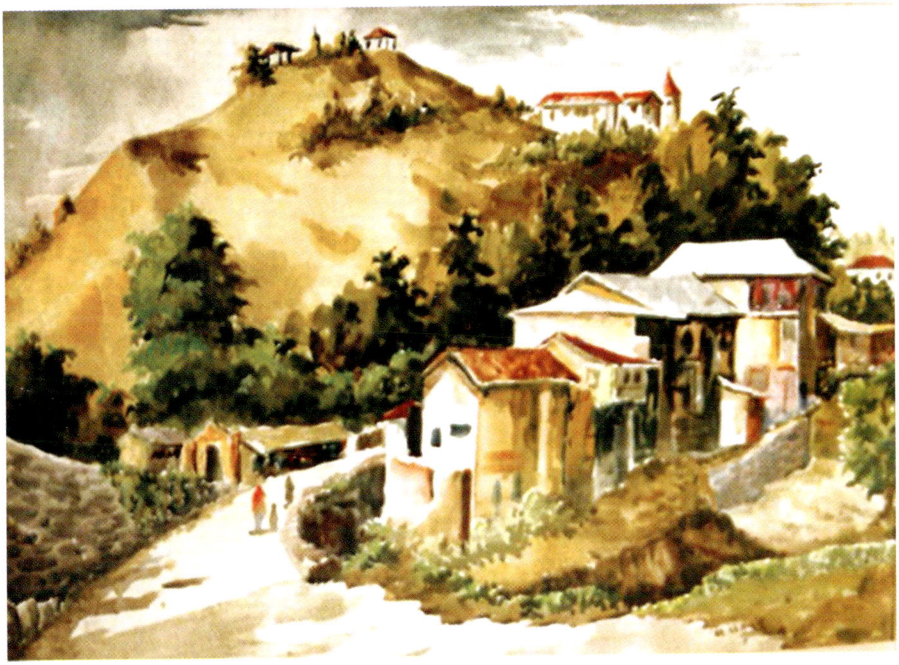

An early landscape

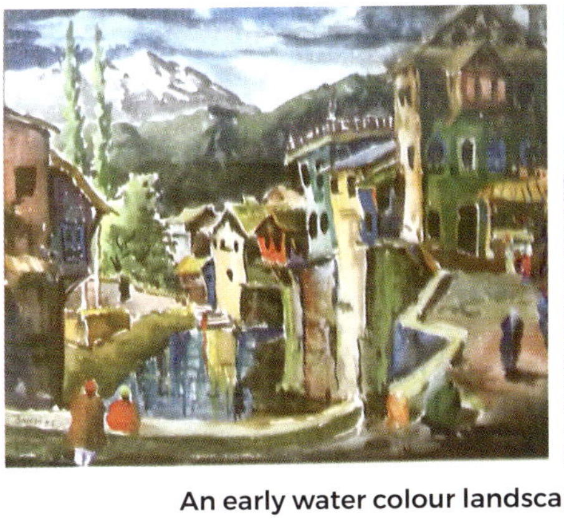

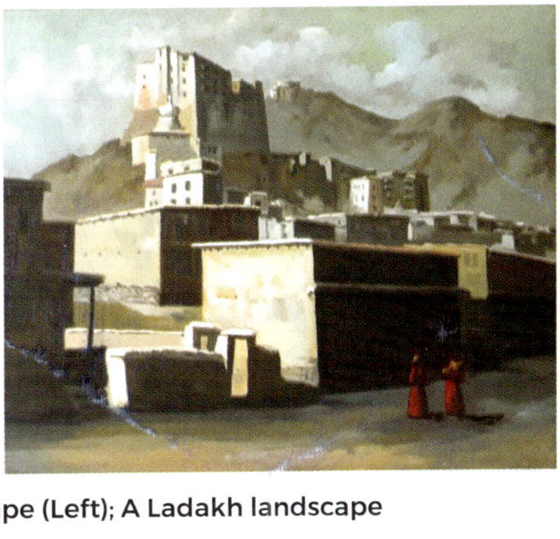

An early water colour landscape (Left); A Ladakh landscape

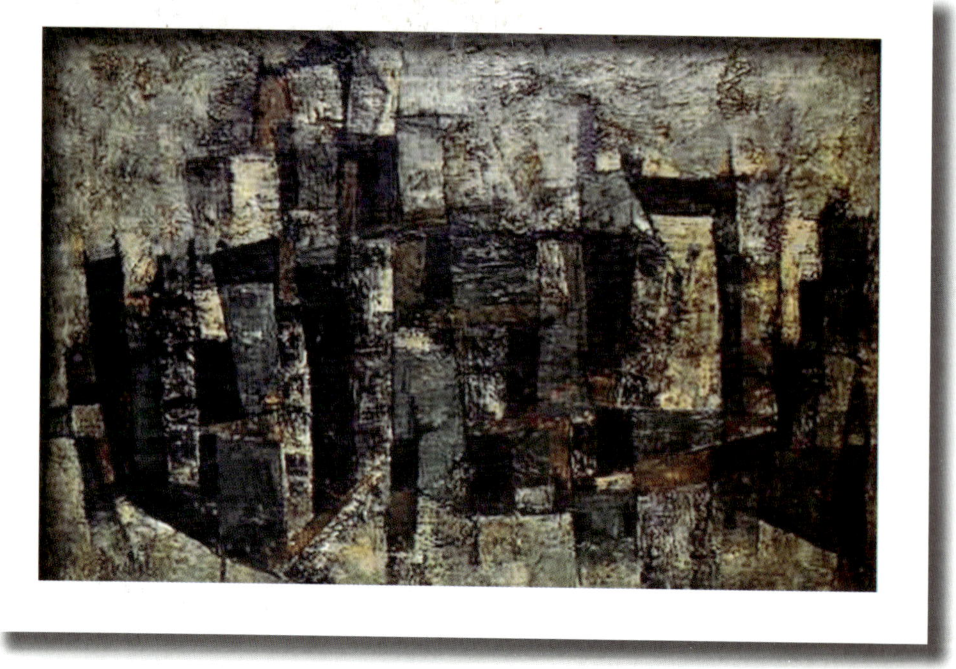

Parimu Abstract

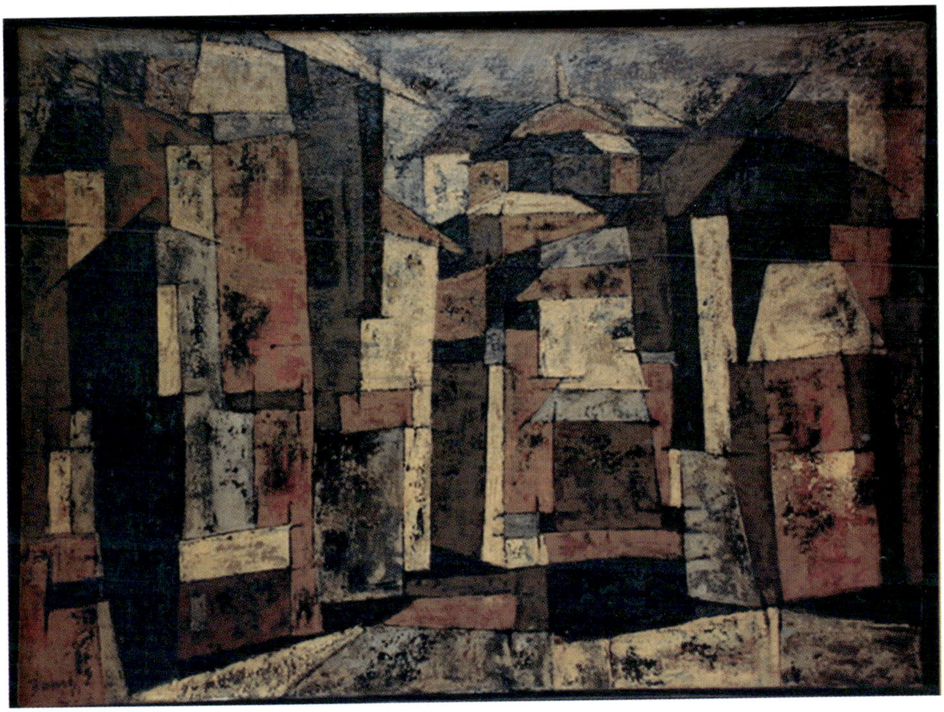

Parimu Abstract Cluster of Houses

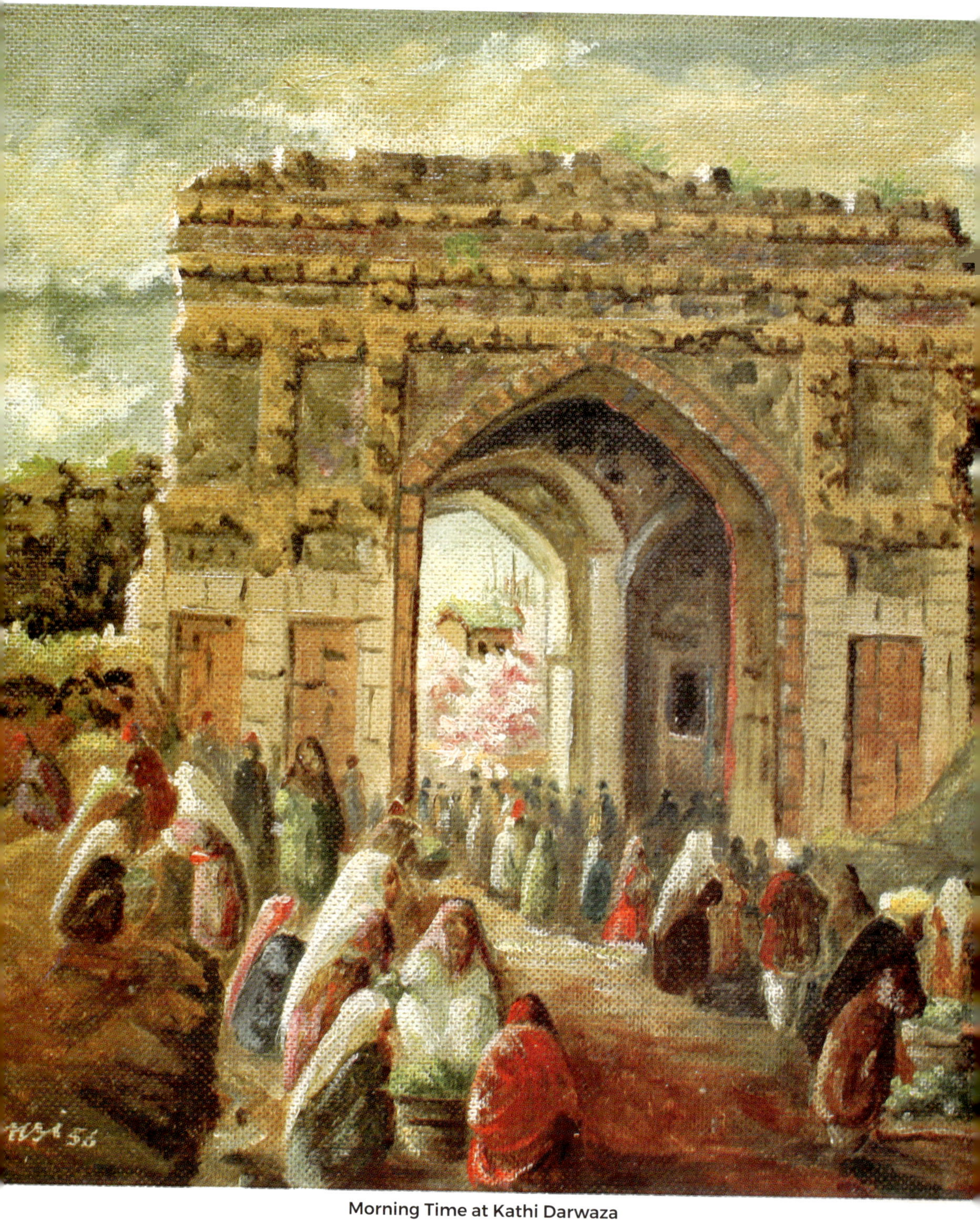

Morning Time at Kathi Darwaza

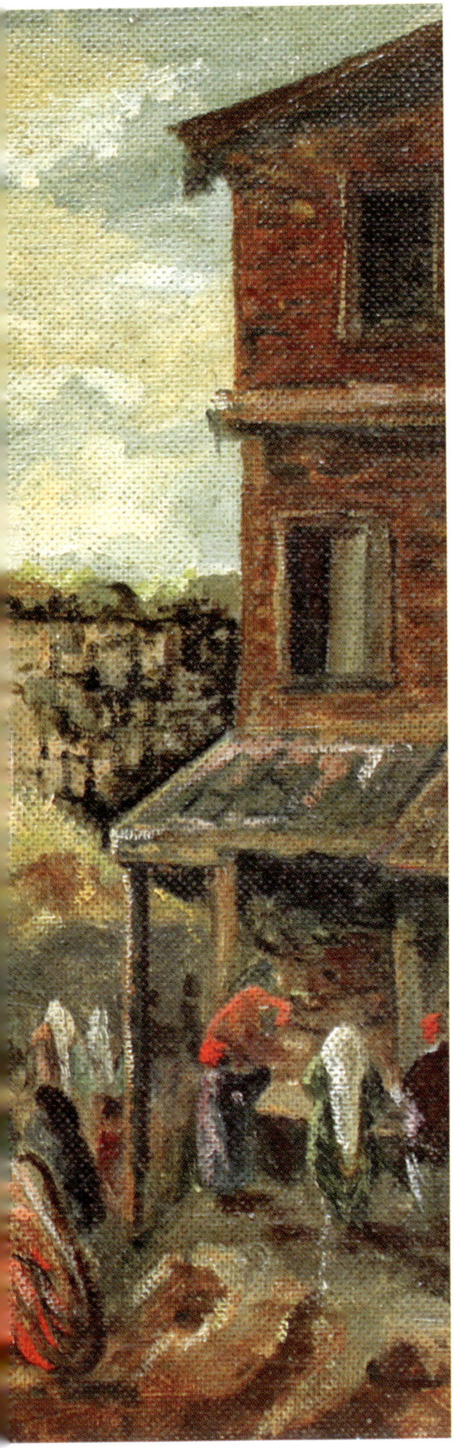

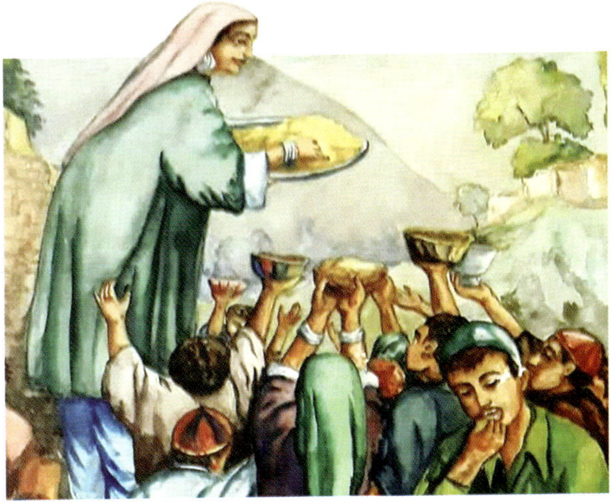

The Tahar Distribution

'Wailing Women' or 'Tahar' (Yellow rice) Distribution' reflect the culture of Kashmir. He had the material to impress artists on the national scene. I have watched him at work. His long fingers used to wield the brush like a violinist and surgeon combined in one. Unfortunately, those long fingers got afflicted with arthritis once he returned from some Gulf assignment. After the displacement from Kashmir, his last exhibition was held in Delhi. M K Raina, the well-known theatre personality, and I helped him to set up that exhibition at the Sridharni Art Gallery. It was comparable to any of the greatest exhibitions in the world. Many people, artists and art connoisseurs visited that exhibition.

Kashmir had enough to inspire Bansi Parimu. His initial inspiration came from the natural beauty of his native land. Picturesque views with hills, meadows, mountains, valleys, trees, and lakes, apart from changing seasons and the variety in flora and fauna attracted him. He started his artistic journey with Kashmir's landscapes that could be ascribed to painter and poet D N Walli's initial influence on him. Whether depicting landscapes or human figures, Bansi Parimu's formal vocabulary was consistent during this period. The use of colours and a strong flavour of the rootedness of his art is visible in the paintings that depict the morning scene of 'Kathi Darwaza' or 'Tahar Distribution' (yellow rice distribution) and many more similar works.

KASHMIR'S RICH CULTURE ON CANVAS

Bansi Parimu loved painting Kashmir's pluralistic and shared culture. He remained involved in this activity for some time before he moved to figurative abstracts. The three paintings that were widely admired included:

TAHAR (YELLOW RICE) DISTRIBUTION

Tahar or yellow rice cooked with turmeric powder, common salt and laced with clarified butter or heated mustard oil is a symbol of Kashmir's composite culture. Both Pandits and Muslims cook it. Kashmiri Pandits cook it on birthdays or for offering it to deities as thanksgiving. They distribute this Tahar among the neighbours on birthdays and carry it to the Ashrams of saints. They do not use onions for preparing Tahar rice.

Tahar is also prepared by Kashmiris when something untoward was expected to happen but luckily did not happen, or someone was saved from some trouble or misfortune or accident. I vividly remember how promptly our ladies cooked yellow rice or Tahar as a thanksgiving to the almighty. I remember my mother preparing Tahar rice and feeding the birds after moving the yellow rice-laden plate two or three times over my head. At that time, she used to say softly: Let every evil be away from you.

Muslims also prepare it for Thanksgiving or Shukraana and Niyaaz. Some families invariably cook it on Fridays and carry it to the mosques or Ziyarats for distribution after prayers. Kashmiri Muslims add shallots (*Praan* in Kashmiri) to it and cook large quantities and quite often distribute it among the people on the roadside.

MORNING TIME AT KATHI DARWAZA

The gate known as Kathi Darwaza is part of one of the last remnant sections of the 16th century wall around the Hari Parbat hill, built by Emperor Akbar. The purpose was to settle residents of Srinagar to the new fortified township known as Nagar Nagor. He also built a fort on the top of the Sharika Parbat hill, also known as Koh-e-Maraan. Later, in 1808 CE, this fort was extensively renovated by the then Afghan governor of Kashmir. Even to this day, three stone gates can be seen on this dilapidated stone wall. Sangeen Darwaza faces the Sharika Temple on the Hari Parbat hill while the Kathi Darwaza faces the Chhati Padshahi Gurudwara. Another gate known as Bachhi Darwaza was dilapidated and has been put to extensive repairs now. This gate faces the shrine of Maqdoom Sahib. In a way, Kathi Darwaza with three shrines of three different faiths around it became a pivotal spot in Kashmir's pluralistic tradition and culture of tolerance that received a serious setback during the armed militancy of the 1990s.

During the morning hours, one would see the worshippers of all the faiths conversing happily near the Kathi Darwaza. The vegetable market outside the Kathi Darwaza would welcome every person and entice one to buy fresh vegetables. Women from the Pandit and the Muslim families could be seen communicating happily and sharing joys and sorrows while buying the vegetables in this market.

My friend, Poet Ayaz Rasool Nazki, has written the poem *Panun Kashmir* or Our Own Kashmir, on the morning scene at the Kathi Darwaza. The poem describes the sturdy bonds of affection and goodwill that existed between the Pandits and the Muslims in the Kashmir valley before 1990. The poem narrates how a Muslim vegetable seller keeps aside the fresh stock of the Dal vegetables for a fatherly Kashmiri Pandit buyer who was expected to come after performing his daily pooja at the Sharika Temple nearby. The poem also conveys how a Pandit would advise his fellow Muslim colleague in the office not to misuse G P fund savings, while secretly helping him with cash, or how a butcher felt reluctant to sell mutton to his Pandit buyer on the Ashtami Day. Here is the English translation of the poem:

OUR OWN KASHMIR

Early in the morning,
after his daily worship and prayers,
the Pandit would come to Hari Parbat
and then to Kathi Darwaza.
A woman vegetable seller from the Dal lake
would call him,
Sir! this way!
Sir, when you left your home,
your wife must have surely told you
to buy,
green gourds from the Dal Lake,
two bundles of carrots,
some brinjals,
some tasty green leafy Haak (collard greens),
four bundles of Pumbutchh,[1]
Sir, all these here,
Sir, here separately for you to carry along.
Well, that is fine my daughter.
May you prosper!

1 Pumbutchh : The fresh variety of seeds held inside a green shell of a lotus flower is called Pumbutchh in the Kashmiri language. These seeds are soft, white and sweet to taste. About twenty seeds are generally held on a spongy green bulb. Once exposed to heat and air, the shell of the seeds turns hard and black. The soft white seed inside it dries up and changes its colour to yellowish-brown. In Kashmir, these lotus seeds are eaten raw. A good amount of dried lotus seeds are used by the Kashmiri Pandits as the Homa Samagri (material for burning in the sacred fire or Yajna Agni).

May your husband live long!
May you have sufficient to eat!'
And then at 10 am,
the Pandit would enter his office,
and on the top of his files,
would suddenly notice an application from Mohammad Shafi.
There and then he would call for Mohammad Shafi
and say to him,
G P Fund is never spent like this,
while secretly,
handing over twelve hundred
rupees from his own pocket,
a secret
that none would know.
At 5 pm, the Pandit would move out of his office
towards his home,
buy the latest English newspaper,
published from New Delhi
from a vendor on the Residency Road.
Reaching his own Mohalla,
near Agha Hamaam locality,
enter a butcher's shop,
How are you dear Qadda?[2]
Is all going well?
Yes Sir, all well.
My pleasure to serve,
please order what you want.
Dear, give me
a Paav (250 gm) from the upper leg portion.
Sir! Today is Ashtami,[3]
don't you remember?

2 Qadda: A short name used for Ghulam Qadir in Kashmir.

3 Ashtami: The eighth day of the Bikrami calendar considered auspicious by the Hindus. Kashmiri Pandits do not consume any non-vegetarian food on certain days, specifically on Tuesday, Ashtami and many other auspicious days. Kashmiri Pandit ladies eat only one meal on Ashtami. They cook this meal only after cleaning the kitchen and washing all the utensils afresh. Ashtami fast in a Kashmiri Pandit household is a part of their age-old tradition and culture.

SEMI-REALISM AND FIGURATIVE ABSTRACTS

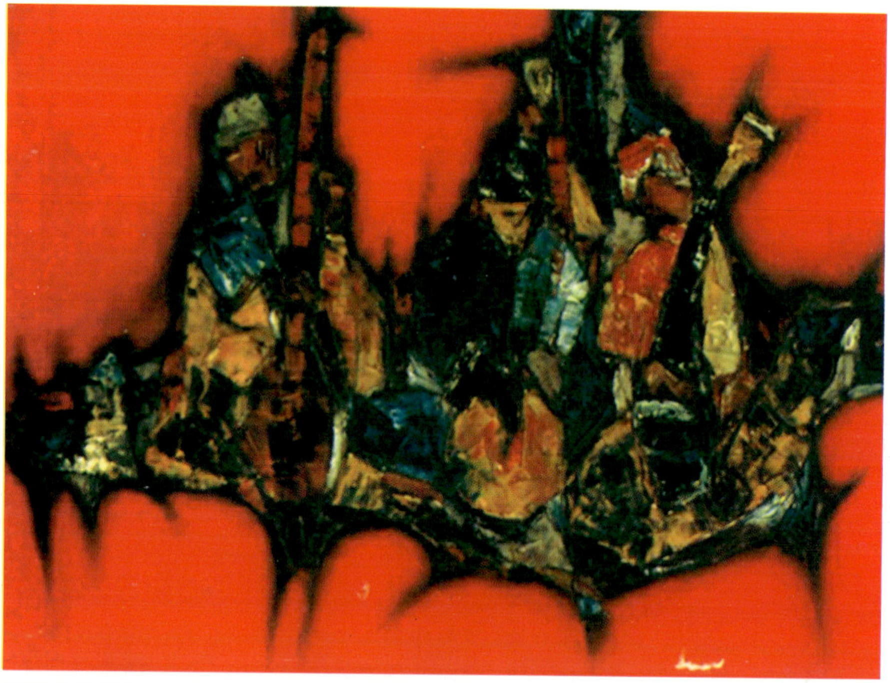

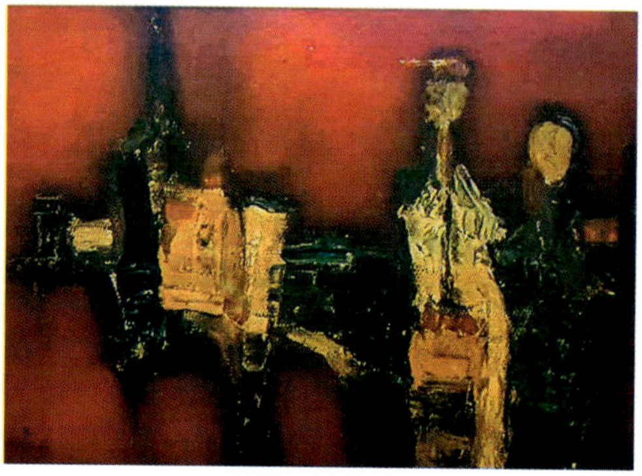

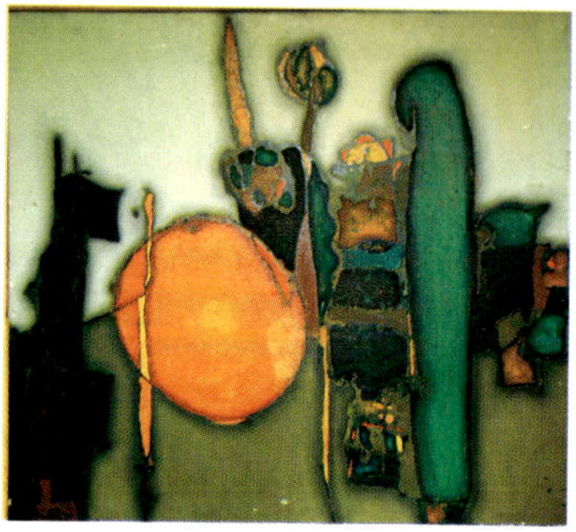

'Figurative Art' is a term for art that refers to the representation of the human figure, however, altered or distorted. It is often applied to paintings and sculptures made after artists re-introduced elements of the human body into abstract styles in the late nineteenth century, including in work by Pablo Picasso, Alberto Giacometti, Francis Bacon, and Lucian Freud.

Many art critics believe that there is nothing like semi-realism. It is either realism or abstract. However, one tends to believe that in semi-realistic art, qualities are overstated, simplified, or stylised to add artistic flair to the work. Such scope is not found in realism. Whatever it be, one cannot ignore Parimu's semi-realism and figurative work which happens to be unique in its conception and presentation. His painting titled 'Three Musicians' done in figurative abstract format was much appreciated.

Writing in the *The Telegraph* of 4 April 1992, art critic Suneet Chopra says, 'Figurative art is conscious communication. But it is all the more powerful when what is felt is something deeply rooted in the artist. Then the structure, the palette, abstract forms and figurative references all blend in his best works that makes Bansi Parimu 's work memorable'.

Commenting on Parimu's work after a commemorative exhibition was organised by Dhoomimal Art Gallery in February 1992, noted art critic Keshav Malik wrote for the *Times of India* issue of 26 February:

> Though the exhibition is timely, the painter's work scattered all over J&K and here, needs a better, a more thoroughly selected exhibition. It represents a body of work which he did after those red patches (Smeared Snows) but also compositions which celebrate eternal life, the best of these later works honour, in their own terms – the terms of contemporary art space – the spirit of delight which is reflected at its tantalizing best in the valley and its waters. A nature in love – soft and gentle – which once brought about a feeling of trust in its humans. The painter would most assuredly have meditated in those famed lakes

that in the summer are like vast sheets of broken glass, and on the poplars that look like fingers pointing towards the sun high above the brightly curved hills. Parimu's work then is a mathematical token of the soft fall of the Shikara oars – its slow progress emphasising the quality of sacredness one associates with things of the risen spirit.

THE PURE ABSTRACTS

Definition of Abstract Art varies. It tries to encompass all things at the

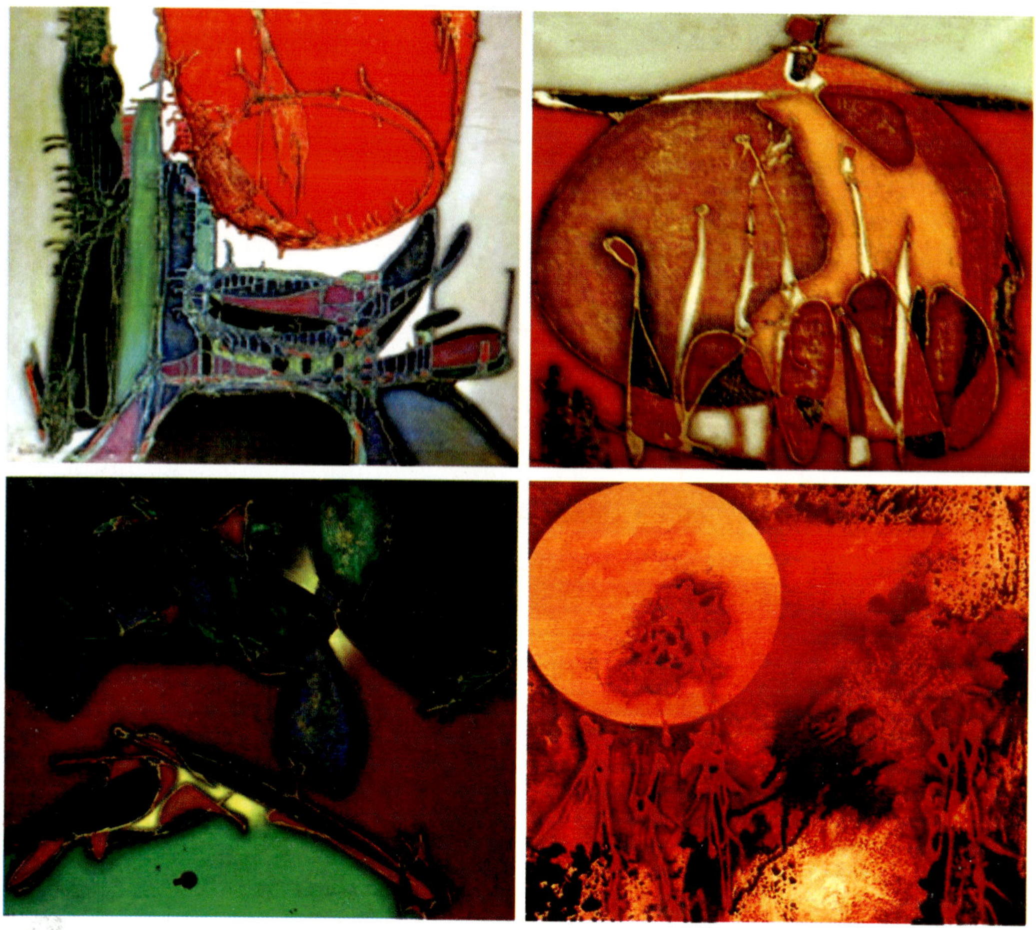

Pure Abstracts

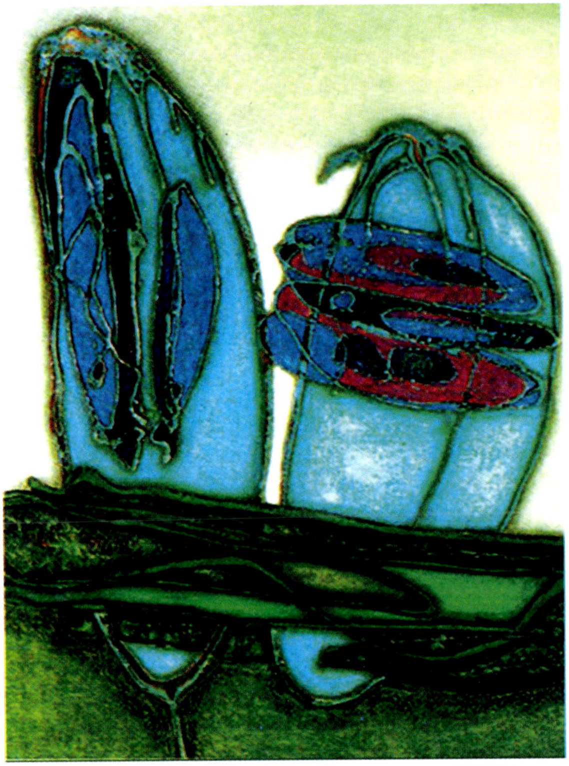

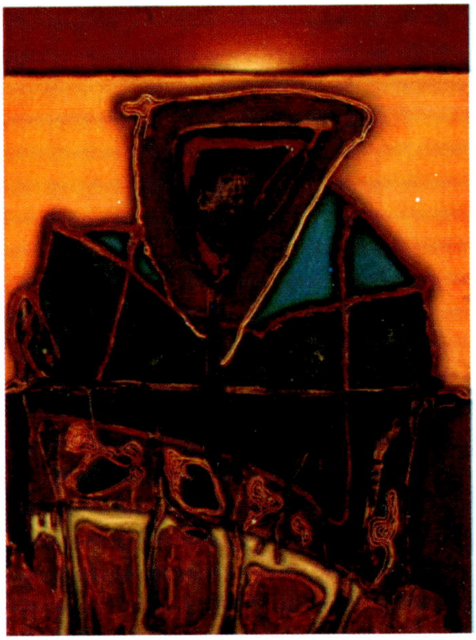

Pure Abstracts

same time yet retain the individualism of each piece of work unique to its own time and context. Pablo Picasso said, 'There is no abstract art. You must always start with something. Afterwards, you can remove all traces of reality'.

For Arshile Gorky, 'Abstraction allows man to see with his mind what he cannot see physically with his eyes'.

And Albert Camus had this caveat, 'If it adapts itself to what the majority of our society wants, art will be a meaningless recreation'.

A brochure at the Princeton University Art Museum in the US defines figurative abstract art thus, 'From the exaggerated proportions of ancient fertility goddesses to the exacting mathematical ratios of the classical Greek canon, the human body has long been used to represent cultural values and intellectual systems in art. However, as abstract painting rose in prominence following World War II, representations of the figure largely disappeared from avant-garde painting, and the presence of the body was subsumed by the physicality of gestural brush strokes'.

Another art-related journal published from the US says, 'The dominant artistic movement in the 1940s and 1950s, abstract expressionism was the first to place New York City at the forefront of international modern art. The associated artists developed greatly varying in stylistic approaches but shared a commitment to abstract art that powerfully expresses personal convictions and profound human values. They championed bold, gestural abstraction in all mediums, particularly large painted canvases'.

Artists the world over have embraced abstraction as a meaningful alternative to the depiction of realistic space and form. Many artists consider abstract art as egalitarian since a viewer's appreciation in this style does not depend on learned knowledge of history or literature. History of abstract art leads us to believe that the Russian artist, Wassily Kandinsky (1866-1944), was the first to exhibit his abstract watercolour painting 'Untitled' in 1911. Some art historians believe that Hilma af Klint (1862-1944), a Swedish artist, was the first to experiment with abstraction in art. She is reported to have done about 190 abstracts in late nineteenth century. Hilma af Klint's 'The Ten Biggest' (oil and tempera on paper) is an abstract painting done in 1907. During the same period, we also come across French avant-garde artist, Francis Picabia, doing abstract paintings. So, what started in the late nineteenth century as experimentation finally became a genre adopted by many artists throughout the world in the twentieth century.

In India, this genre was also extensively used by S H Raza, Ram Kumar, Tyeb Mehta, M F Husain, Prabhakar Kolte, V S Gaitonde, S K Bakre, Shobha Broota, Biren De, Satish Gujral, P Khemraj, Devyani Krishna, Akbar Padamsee, Bimal Dasgupta, Sachida Nagdev, Nasreen Mohamedi, J Swaminathan and many others during the twentieth century.

After experimenting with various forms, Parimu was finally drawn towards abstraction. His abstracts are a combination of organic designs, patterns, swirling shapes, colours, and steadfast consistencies. This consistency is reflected in every painting and also in his entire portfolio of work under this genre. In abstract art, Parimu demonstrates a flair for green, blue, red, and yellow colours that are warm and conspicuous. And Parimu has never tried to infuse dullness in his colours.

In Parimu's abstracts, you may not find recognisable objects and given the habit of assigning meaning to what we see, we may end up saying, 'there is nothing to grasp or hold on to' once we see his work. But that is a generalisation and not the truth. The truth is, every abstract that Parimu has done has its basis, form, colour, line, pattern, composition, and process. His work in this genre is an exploration of these formal qualities meant to create a visual experience even for the lay viewer. And then reality is subjective, and it is up to a viewer to define it.

Parimu appears to have understood the new figuration in abstract art. His abstracts are not merely markings, organic shapes, smudges, smatterings, conical ovals, rings, bright colours, blots, drippings, sprays, and squeezes but skilful use of lines, shapes, colours, and pattern to create rhythm on canvas. To a serious viewer, his abstracts also represent newer issues of human civilisation. The rebuff signs that are reflected in some of his abstracts can be construed as serious reflections of what lies in present-day societies on the ground: Glare and emptiness or haze and the deceptive clarity. These abstracts also convey contingency and abandonment of human existence.

Art lovers and connoisseurs, who are familiar with works of Paul Klee, Jackson Pollock, Miquel Barcelo, Julian Schnabel, Clyfford Still, Georg Baselitz, Jean-Paul Riopelle, Agnes Martin, Georges Mathieu, Franz Kline, and Karel Appel will have no issue in appreciating the merit of Parimu's abstracts. One can also include Mark Rothko in this list, although his work differed from other abstract artists, especially the way he diffused paint all over the canvas rather than subjecting it to gestural attacks.

Artists like Jackson Pollock (1912-1956) believed that it was the viewer and not the artist who defined and interpreted the meaning of the abstract expressionist artwork. His work features dynamic and impulsive movement through seemingly messy marks. Quite often, it may look as if he merely throws the paint at the canvas. Convergence is a painting done by Pollock in 1952. This represents his earlier works of abstract expressionism and is considered one of the masterpieces of abstract expressionism. This painting can be seen at Albright-Knox Art Gallery, Buffalo, New York.

Further, we need to know the background of an artist of the abstract genre to be able to appreciate and understand his work in a better way. To some extent, the viewer with the maximum knowledge of the abstract artist and his or her background will most value and comprehend the artwork. Krishna Chaitanya writes about Parimu on page 247-248, in his book, *A History of Indian painting – Modern Period:*

> Bansi Parimu created more complex forms. Linear forms that straddle the frame, creating balancing directional thrusts. The areas of uniform colour have been given soft, pearly finish and isolated by contouring which often suggest the relief of cloisonné

> enamel but without the use of ridges of Impasto. In other areas, mottled effects and textures have been obtained in various ways: light rolling over the ground colour with a different one, using the back of the brush for calligraphic arabesques, using the gauze overlays.

Artist Wasim Mushtaq Wani writes about Parimu's abstract works in his 'Thesis on Modern Art In Kashmir':

> Parimu shares more with the classical formalists like Paul Klee or the Indian abstractionists like Gaitonde, Shanti Dave and Jeram Patel. Except for the un-geometric and often referential mode of Parimu's paintings, his compositional arrangement is also quite close to that of Prabhakar Kolte.

In 1986, Parimu did a one-man show at the Shridharani Art Gallery, New Delhi. About this show, *The Statesman* newspaper's art critic wrote in the 26 February issue:

> Bansi's creative gesture is abstract, but his forms are not abstracted. Certain elements do repeat, orbs, conical ovals or plantain leaf or blades of fans like shapes, sensitised with mixed colour energies by the edges, dripping moves of energy within or penetrative drives of energy from without (orbs) or exuding illusions of depression couched in prominent embodying lines (blades). The work is resonant with strong and divergent rings which in their vertical or diagonal gestures, stops and releases, become highly suggestive of the involvement of time and that penultimate stage when forms begin to show up.

Commenting on the abstracts that Parimu exhibited in the Dhoomimal Art Gallery sometime in December 1988, noted art critic Santo Datta wrote in *The Indian Express* of 31 December, 'As the late

Jaya Appaswamy analysed correctly, the Abstract Art[4] with its new set of pictorial values, came to India around the fifties, not inspired by the contemporary movement of abstract expressionism but was inspired by the works of Kandinsky and Paul Klee. And it struck its first roots in the fifties when pioneers of modern art were breaking down forms to colour planes and spatial arrangements. The works of Bansi Parimu belong to this long line of experiment with a new aesthetic experience. The painter, despite a long spell of disabling arthritis, has been painting with uncanny devotion found usually among religious thinkers. Compared to his earlier paintings, the recent ones are less heavy with coloured wax. In fact, the coloured wax is used for sinuous linear movements, giving total compositional unobtrusive but lively linear accents, the kind we admired in the lacquered Ukiyo-e Woodblock prints of the late 18th and 19th centuries in Japan. Parimu's paintings are more poetic in the line of Kandinsky[5] in their areas of tensions of colours than the linear intellectual whimsies of Paul Klee. In fact, the artist has successfully hidden the structure of tensions between colour fields and linear movements and has given his work a kind of spontaneity, a feeling of fortuitous relationships between different degrees of tensions on the surface. The patient viewer will notice

4 In the US, I found that every university and town has its art museum or gallery with a well-preserved collection of paintings, sculptures, and artefacts. In the Princeton University Art Museum, I found works of some great masters like Pablo Picasso, Vincent Van Gogh, Paul Gauguin, Pissarro, Claude Monet and many more along with many abstracts. I also observed that the abstract language is widely used in installation art. The art installations at the Storm King Art Centre, Mountainville, Cornwall, about 50 km from New York are worth seeing. Many abstract sculptures have been installed in this open-air park of 500 acres. More than 100 large-scale sculptures done by some of the most acclaimed artists of our time, including Alexander Calder, Mark di Suvero, Andy Goldsworthy, Zhang Huan, Maya Lin, Louise Nevelson, Isamu Noguchi, Claes Oldenburg, Richard Serra, and David Smith are on display over there. Maya Lin's 'Storm King Wave Fields' is something unusual to see in art. These 'Wave Fields' have been developed in 2009 over 240,000 sq feet of gravel land and look like ocean waves created out of green grass. At places these green waves rise to 15 feet, then move down, rising once again to create crests and troughs of moving waves. One gets a feeling of being in the mid-sea with waves and waves all around. [See Photos].

5 According to the art manual published by Christie's titled 'Impressionist and Modern Paintings, Drawings and Sculptures (Part I)' for their auction on 13 November 1996 at New York, an abstract painting of Wassily Kandinsky (1866-1944) was put up for sale at a reserve price range of USD 200,000 to 300,000. It was done in watercolour and black ink on paper. In the same auction, an abstract done by Georges Braque (1883-1963) using oil on canvas had a reserve price range of USD 300,000 to 400,000. And a semi-abstract (also known as mechanical art) of Fernand Leger (1881-1955) had a price range of USD 500,000-700,000.

particularly his use of tonality which never dominates the colour areas, instead, the tones always appear subservient to lines which, in their turn, bring in the abstract forms. This has given his paintings the charm of viscosity prints, luminous but not flashy.'

On Bansi Parimu's first death anniversary, 31 July 1992, art critic R S Yadav of The *Hindustan Times* summed up his art in this way:

> Done in abstract vein, Bansi's landscapes unfold before the viewer – the irresistible poetry of colours and an engaging orchestration of lines. Rich in emotional content, they transport the viewer to a different world, a world of Sufi saints or that of the Indian Vaishnavites wherein love and devotion alone rule. Organically structured to perfection, these soul-filling chromatic psalms are a unique experience for the viewer to confront and absorb. These creations of Bansi also release the inner being and rearrange his core with qualitatively different stuff, for these are the outcome of his ordeal before the easel and the canvas .

In his abstracts, Bansi Parimu uses a wide range of colours, including green, blue, red and ochre. His work demands a closer scrutiny and multiple viewing to appreciate it in totality. His abstracts received wide appreciation in the festival of art held in 2003 at Jasubhai Art Gallery, Shanmukhananda Hall in Mumbai. Works of artists like K H Ara, F N Souza, K K Hebbar and Rabindranath Tagore were also on display in this exhibition.

PORTRAITURE

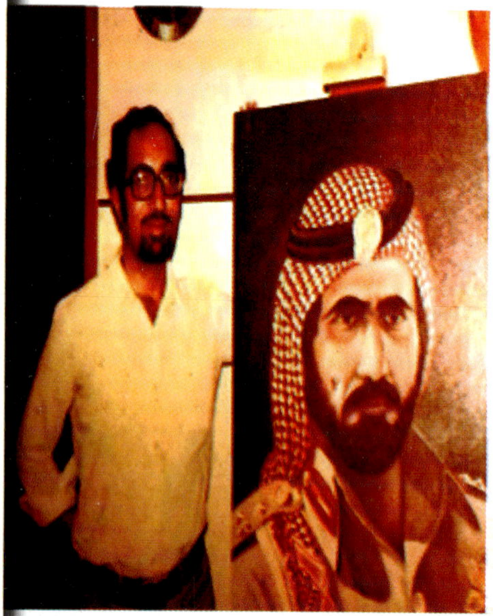

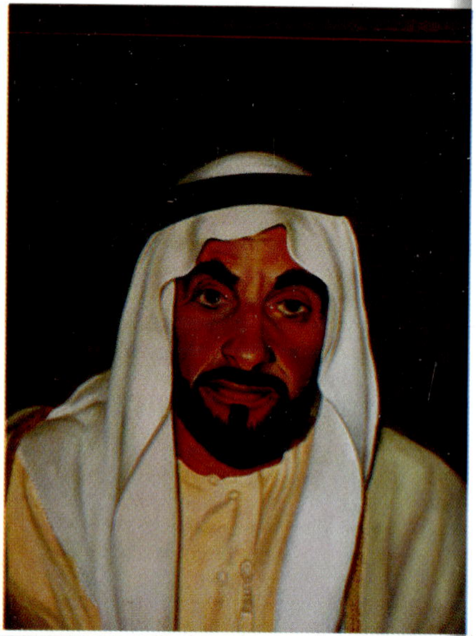

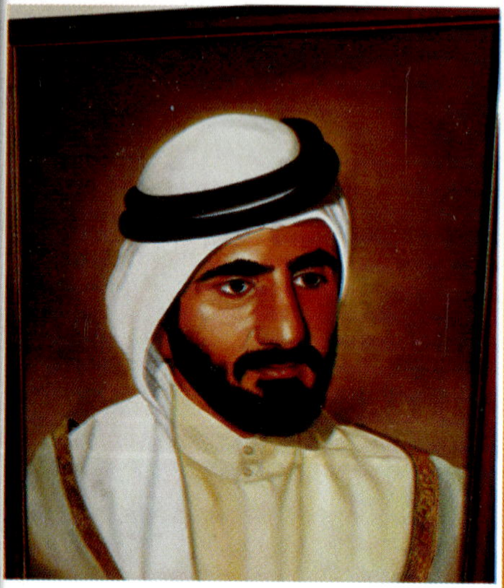

Portraits of members of the UAE royal family Parimu drew during his stint in Dubai.

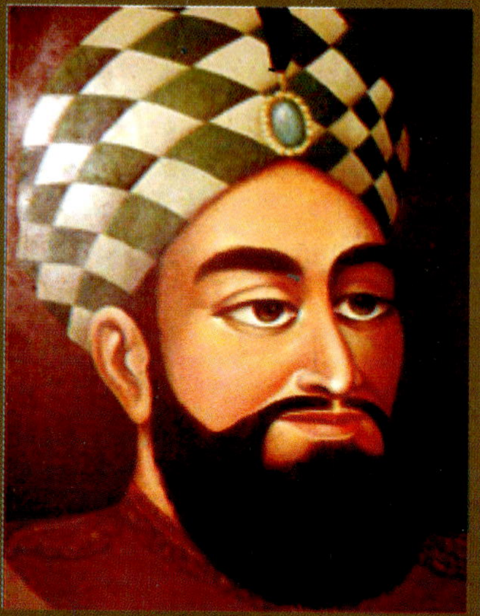

A portarit of Sultan Zainul Abdin

> Every portrait that is painted with feeling is a portrait of the artist, not of the sitter. The sitter is merely the accident, the occasion. It is not he who is revealed by the painter; it is rather the painter who, on the coloured canvas, reveals himself.
>
> **—Oscar Wilde**

Jaya Parimu says that Bansi had also done a self-portrait and a remarkable portrait of his father. He did some portraits for friends and relations too. He also did some impressive portraits of the members of UAE's royal family.

According to Capt S K Tikoo, a close friend from his school days, 'Bansi Parimu did not do much work in this area. I believe he disliked it, but whatever few portraits he painted are outstanding. Look at Parimu's portraits of Zayed Bin Sultan Al Nahayan, the president of the UAE and Shaikh Mohammad Bin Rashid, the ruler of Dubai. I believe he did these portraits in 1977 or 1978, when he was in the Middle East. You will understand his versatility through these portraits. He had also drawn an impressive portrait of Dr Ho Chi Minh when the Vietnamese leader visited India. In fact, he wanted to present the portrait personally to Dr Ho Chi Minh'.

Writer-banker Indu Bushan Zutshi recalls, 'A beautiful portrait of Karl Marx done by Bansi Parimu was in possession of my brother Vijay Zutshi. It was lying in his house at Anantnaag. It was hanging prominently from the wall of his drawing-room. This prized portrait was also lost in the militancy of the 1990s when my brother had to leave Anantnaag in a hurry due to threats from the armed militants. My brother has told me that Bansi Parimu had painted some more portraits of the Russian communist leaders. A few were lying in the shop that he had rented near Habba Kadal bridge in Srinagar city. And one such portrait had been gifted to Pyare Lal Handoo, a minister in the Farooq Abdullah cabinet'.

He was also commissioned by the J&K Academy of Art, Culture, and Languages for drawing portraits of some icons of Kashmir in the fields of art, culture, and politics. The Academy's commission had included one portrait of Sultan Zainul Abdin. I was informed that this portrait was drawn by Parimu simply by using his imaginative brilliance. In his foreword to the book *Kashmiri Language And Poetry of Abdul Ahad Azad*, published by the J &K Academy of Art, Culture, and Languages in 1981, M Y Taing writes, 'In this publication we have published a portrait of the great philanthropist Sultan Zainul Abdin or Budshah, which was created for the Islamic Exhibition of the Academy'.

SCULPTURE

In the January-June 2019 issue of *Miraas*, an English magazine published from New Delhi, Vijay Vishen writes:

> Bansi Parimu's artistic fervour found expression, to a limited extent, in sculpting. The bust of a Kashmiri peasant and the mother and child figurine are his prominent works in this genre. Portraiture also interested him and he was requisitioned by the Academy of Art, Culture, And Languages to do a portrait of Sultan Zain ul Abdin (Budshah), the fourteenth-century ruler of Kashmir. In this portrait, the minute detailing of the turban fabric, embroidery on the collar piece, the colour of the eyes, even the eyebrows and eyelashes, amply demonstrate his versatility as a painter. For his proficiency in portraiture, he was invited by the ruling family of the Gulf Emirates to do several portraits and stayed in the Gulf countries for some time in the late seventies of the last century.

I am unable to say anything definite about the extent of commissioned work that Bansi Parimu did for the J&K Academy of Art, Culture, and Languages beyond what has been stated above, as no clear details could be obtained in spite of my hectic efforts.

A PAINTER USING THE ENCAUSTIC TECHNIQUE

The twentieth century saw the rebirth of the ancient encaustic technique in painting. Encaustic (enkaustikos) is a word of Greek origin meaning 'to heat or burn in'. Encaustic consists of natural bees-wax and resin. The medium can be used alone for its transparency or adhesive qualities or pigmentation. Over a period of time, the surface of a painting done in this medium retains its gloss. Bansi Parimu was possibly the first artist in Kashmir to experiment with this technique. The Austria-based artist, Kapil Kaul, says:

> A progressive and inquisitive mind like Bansi Parimu could conceive new ideas that supported and inspired his vision. When and how he came to transform his painting technique into encaustic is yet to be ascertained but his participation in shows with paintings done in this technique should be able to provide clarity. He had discovered for himself an unconventional method of painting that would give a wide range of possibilities in achieving diverse shapes and varied forms, revealing the visual magic of his world on one side and exposing it to manifold interpretations on the other. Parimu's method of using bees-wax was altogether different.
>
> Encaustic is a centuries-old technique of using hot bees-wax with pigments for painting. Some of the oldest examples appear in the 6th century painted icons in Egypt. A painter in the US, Jasper Johns (born 1930), known for his painting series of the American flag, worked in encaustic technique. Parimu prepared hot fluid bees-wax, heated in a canister within a water bath and mixed with certain resins, mastic, and turpentine – in a formula that remains his secret. The technical use of bees-wax needed to be mastered. It is not to be mistaken with ordinary candle or paraffin wax. In order to guarantee the durability of his artwork, he initially experimented with the ingredients. In a state of utmost concentration, he splashed and spread the hot molten wax on a stretched canvas laid on the floor. He tilted the canvas to control

its flow. As the wax cooled down and froze, it stuck permanently to the surface. At this stage, the frozen splash of yellowish looking wax on the canvas appeared like a relief. After this step, the main work of painting in oils followed. So as not to damage the soft wax layer, he used soft sable hair brushes which are usually used for watercolour painting. Bristle hair brushes used generally for oil painting would have been too hard for the wax layer. Right from the wax splash to the application of colour, Parimu's painting underwent a complete metamorphosis.

In 1972, I was witness to a painting demonstration to which Parimu was invited by the local Institute of Music and Fine Arts in Srinagar. He had taken with him the bees-wax solution in a canister which was heated before embarking on the creative demonstration.

The splash of wax froze, resembling a geographic topography that he painted in a reduced colour scheme of complementary colours, choosing orange and green. He explained his impulse of the painting, saying he had a feeling of intruding as a stranger into that room full of young students. Hence the painting was titled 'Intrusion'.

TABLEAUS, MURALS AND INSTALLATIONS

Bansi Parimu was also engaged by the J&K government for preparing the State's tableaus that were displayed on the Republic Day parade at New Delhi. One such tableau was done by him during Jawahar Lal Nehru's tenure as the prime minister. Nehru was very happy to see the concept and design of the tableau. He not only admired the work but also invited Bansi Parimu to Teen Murti over a cup of tea. In this meeting, Parimu presented a painting to Nehru.

Parimu did some large murals and installations in the Middle East where he stayed for about two years during the late seventies of the last century. He worked in Oman, Muscat, Doha, Dubai, and some other places.

AWARDS, SHOWS, EXHIBITIONS

Bansi Parimu was not only a respected artist in Kashmir, he was widely known in the world of Indian modern art. He had many friends abroad in the international world of art. His name and fame spread as a young artist and his collection of awards began in the fifties.

AWARDS

Bansi Parimu received 'The 1955 Industrial Exhibition (Srinagar) 1st Prize' early in his career as an artist. 'The J&K Academy Exhibition 1st Prize' (1960-1968-1969-1970 and 1971) came to him in the next two decades. The 'Madhya Pradesh Kala Parishad Award (1961)' , 'Tagore Exhibition Award' at Amritsar and Kolkata (1961), 'Indian Academy of Art (Amritsar) Award' (1961), 'AIFACS, New Delhi Award' (1964), 'Academy of Fine Arts, Kolkata Award' (1965) all were awarded to him during his most prolific years as an artist. 'Gold Medal and Governor's Award' was presented posthumously to him in 1994.

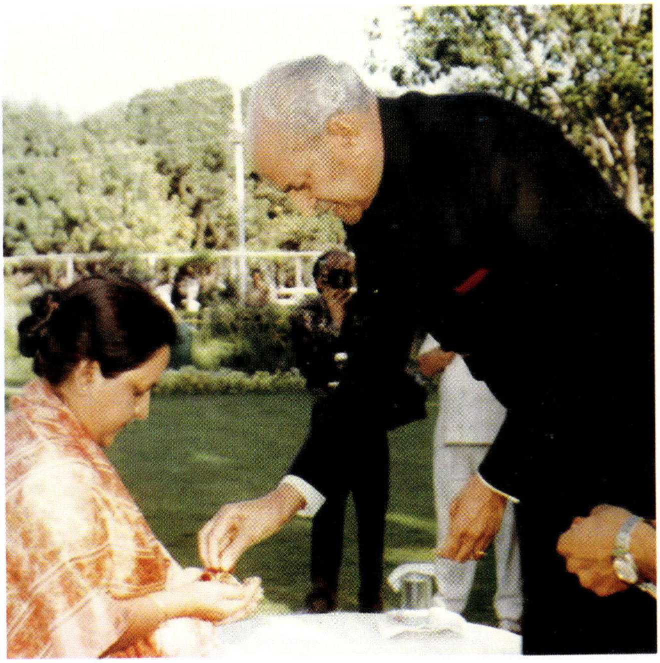

Jaya Parimu receiving award from Governor, J&K in 1994

EXHIBITIONS

The sixties and seventies were also the decades when he held most shows of his work. Some key exhibition held by Bansi Parimu include: the Progressive Artists Association Exhibition of 1952 in Srinagar; J&K Artists Group Exhibition in 1963; Kashmir Art Society Exhibition in 1957; Five Painters, Srinagar Exhibition in 1963; Bombay and New Delhi Exhibitions in 1964.

He participated in many 'All India Exhibitions' from 1958 held at Srinagar, Amritsar, Hyderabad, Kolkata, Mumbai, and other places. He also joined the National Exhibition of Art and Lalit Kala Akademi Exhibitions regularly from 1962.

He held many one-man shows in Srinagar and outside the State: Ambala 1954, New Delhi 1959, 1960, 1965, 1973, 1975, 1986, 1987, 1988 and 1990, Bombay 1963, 1974, 1982 and 1986, Lucknow 1964 and 1965, Ahmedabad 1969, Kolkata 1959 and 1966.

He participated in the 'Indian Art Exhibition 1972' held in San Francisco (USA), The Third Triennale India (1974), 'International Exhibition of Art 1977' held in Copenhagen, 'British Council Art Exhibition 1977' held in Dubai, 'The LKA National Camp 1987' held at Lucknow and 'The Ankara Biennale 1988' held in Turkey.

A commemorative exhibition of Bansi Parimu's work was organised by the Dhoomimal Art Gallery, New Delhi in February 1992. This show drew rave reviews in the national press. A commentary cum review on this show was written by noted art critic, Keshav Malik, which was published in the Times of India of 26 February 1992.

His family also held a 'Retrospective Show' of his work at the Nehru Centre, Kala Ghoda, Mumbai in December 2001. This show was attended by many leading artists and connoisseurs of art. The exhibition showcased various works of the artist done in figurative and pure abstract language. It was widely covered by print and electronic media. Jaya Parimu recalls, "Many Mumbai based artists visited the exhibition. People from the film world too visited and spent time seeking details. We had not sent out invitations and visitors dropped in of their own. People like Govind Nihalani, Pramod Navalkar, Bakul Patel and Mahesh Bhatt also came. Mahesh Bhatt wanted to know what was being depicted by showing a Muslim lady with blood trickling down from above. I had to explain that Parimu felt that women were the real sufferers of the ongoing militancy in the Kashmir valley. I explained that the painting was depicting a mother wailing at the death of her son who had been lured into the armed militancy. Mahesh Bhatt also sought intricate details of the exodus and its impact on Parimu's work."

In 2001, a retrospective exhibition of his work was also held in Dubai.

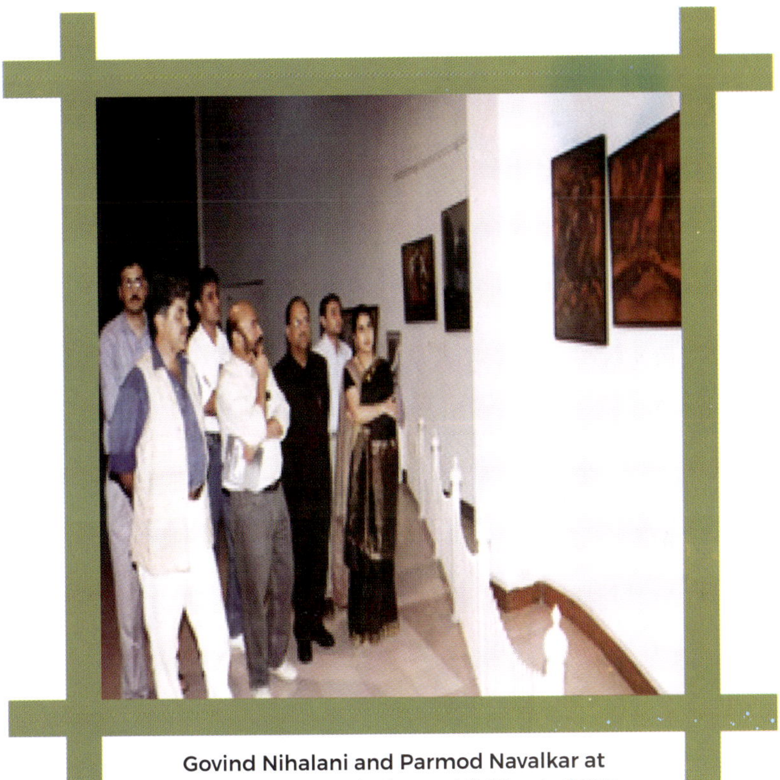

Govind Nihalani and Parmod Navalkar at Bansi Parimu's painting exhibition in 2001

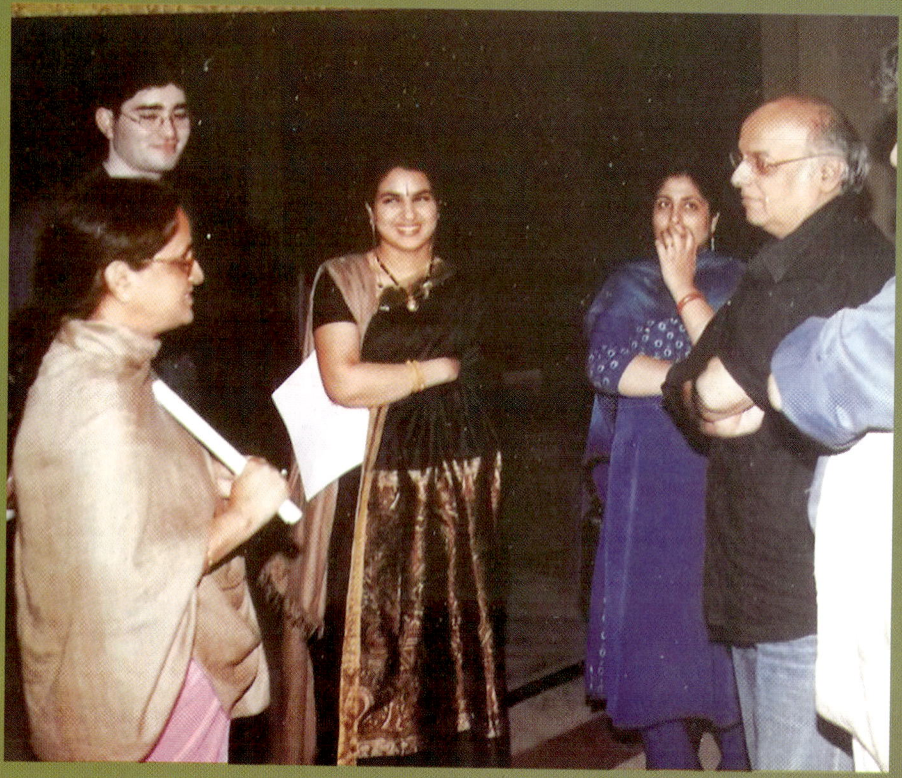

Mahesh Bhatt at Bansi Parimu's paintings exhibition in 2001

THE LAST PHASE OF PARIMU'S WORK AND EXILE

A work of art which did not begin in emotion is not art
—Paul Cézanne

IN THE WAKE of armed militancy in Kashmir, Bansi Parimu was forced to leave the valley and live in exile. Leaving Kashmir was not easy for him. It meant moving away from a culture evolved over five thousand years. No man is born twice, and no man can live on memories. And no flowering and fragrant plant grows in the heat and dust of the alien lands, should it be uprooted. Cobwebs of Apathy, Smeared Snows, The Red Divide , Red Knows No Creed, Flying Kangri, Exodus I, Exodus II, Charging Rams and many more are creations of this deep-rooted feeling of his homelessness and the bloodshed in his native land. The painful dislocation had a perceptible influence on his health and work.

THE GRIEF WITHIN

There was always an amount of pensive grief in Parimu. Parimu lost his mother when he was barely ten years of age. The mother's loss for a child is bound to create some deep inadequacy within. The torment got reflected in his work. He never abandoned painting Kashmiri women. Even before the 1990s, he painted their pain, gloom, silence, helplessness, and hope. He painted elderly Burqa-clad women in conversation on the road. He painted women sharing joys and sorrows of life. He also painted women in an assembly sharing grief and wailing.

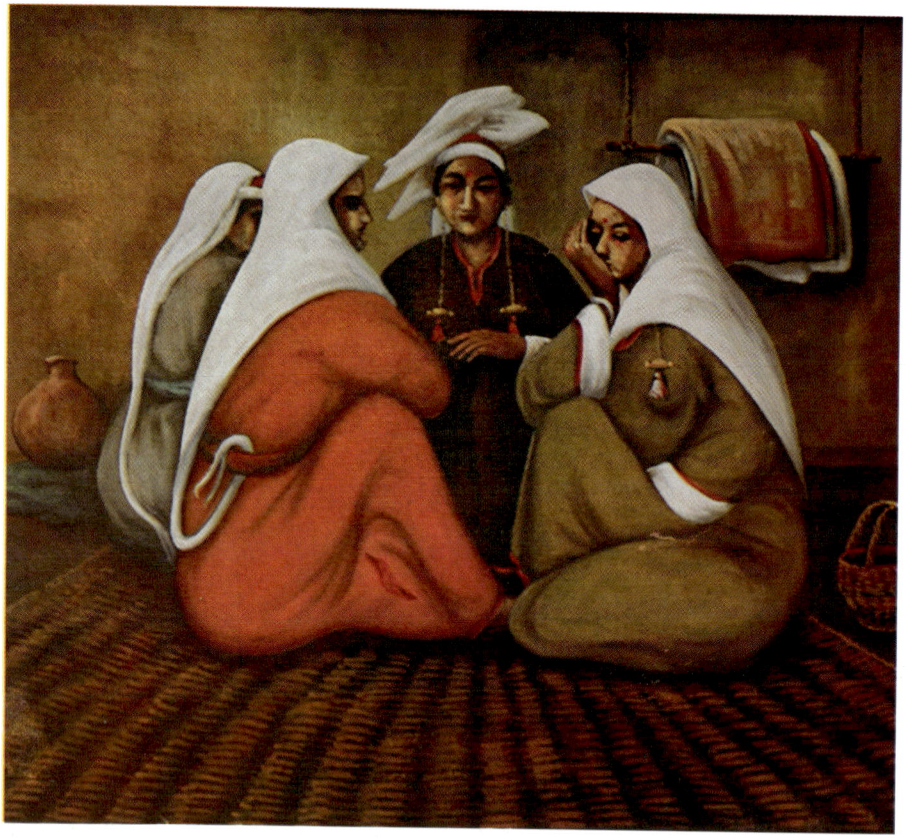

The Grief Within

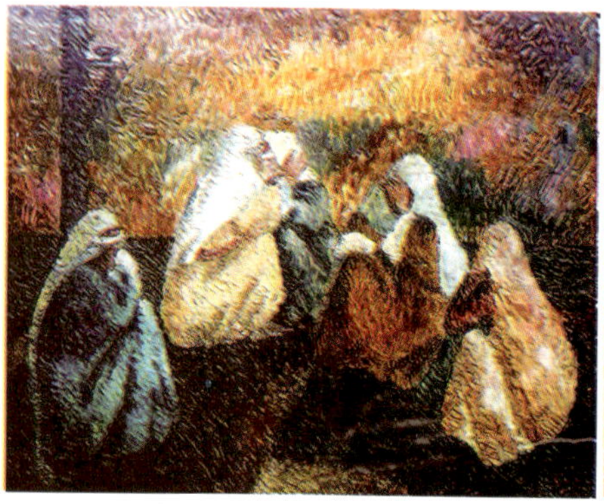

The wailing Women

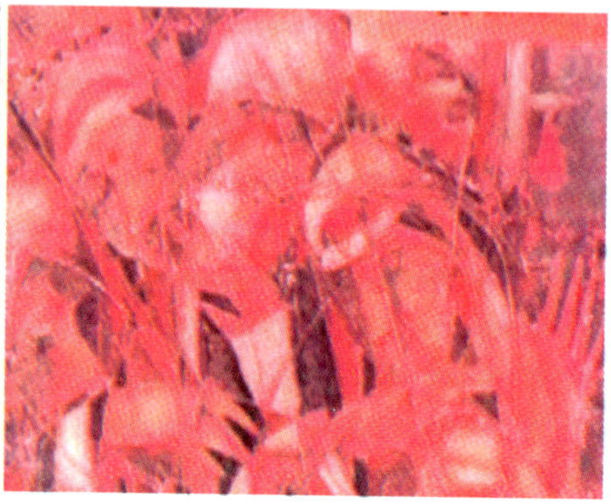

Cobwebs of Apathy

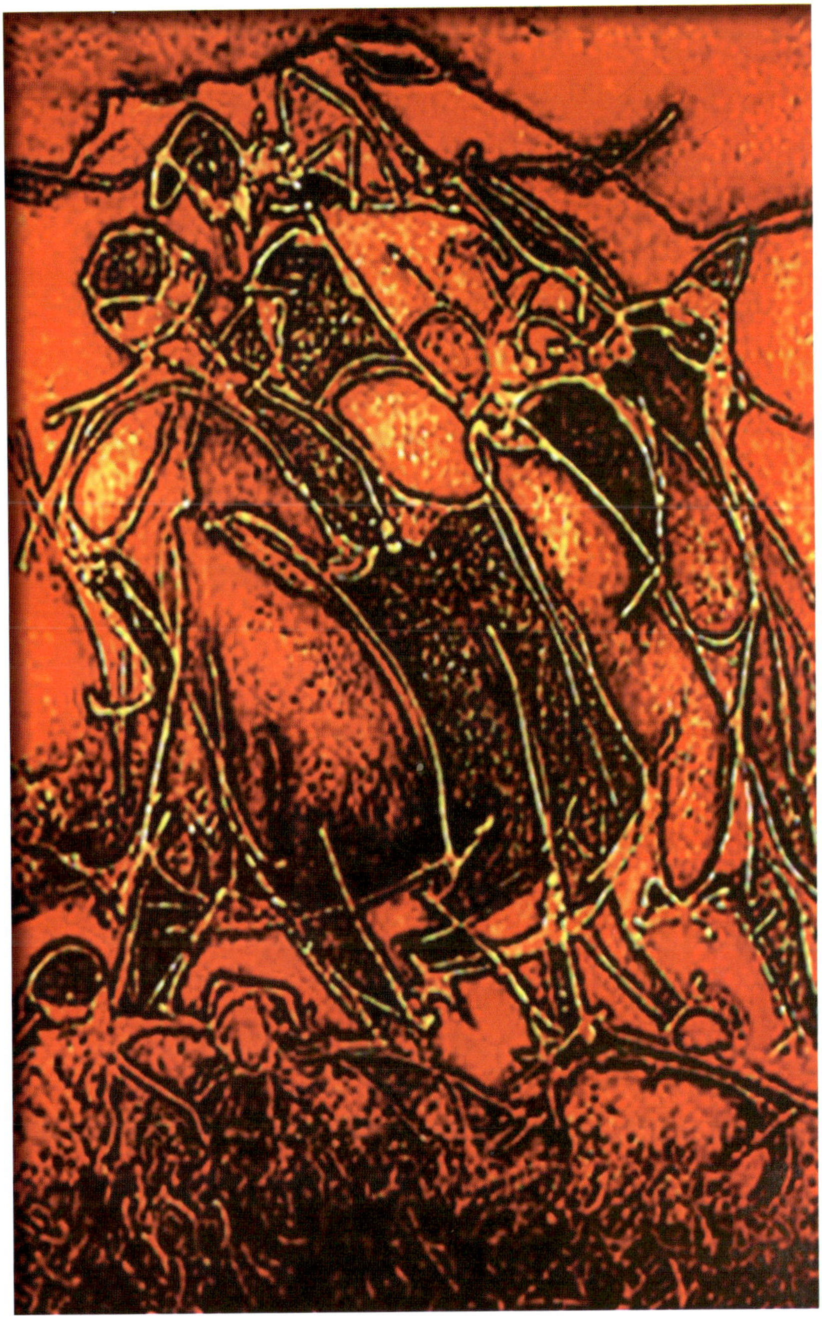

A figurative abstract depicting 'Exodus'

The 'Wailing Women' and 'The Grief Within' were the result of some deep childhood impressions on his mind. One has been done with a knife while the other is a brushwork.

Grieving women, a pitcher of water, a fire pot (Kangri), a Pheran (dress), a clothesline for hanging clothes (Villinj in Kashmiri), Taranga (women's headgear) and a dry hay mat (Voguv in Kashmiri) are visible in the painting, The Grief Within. This painting is very close to Kashmir's recent past. After 1990, he again painted pheran-clad Kashmiri women bound by tradition, simplicity, and sincerity.

These women form the pivot of a dwindling tribe from the snow-capped hills. Accustomed to breezes and brooks, thrown into hot, humid and dusty plains, these women are victims of the disintegrating and crumbling joint family structure. They live with a deep sense of loss on all fronts and carry a profound feeling of homelessness compounded by the loss of identity. For them, life has nothing more to offer except memories. These women keep suffering on all fronts yet never hesitate in comforting others.

The Kashmiri Poet, Ghulam Nabi Firaq, sympathises with these hapless women and expresses his feelings in these lines:

Yetie chhana saayil khaali neraan
Aesh pheir kenh chhiy hargaa laganaai,
soruyi vonamus ti chhum pheraan
akh kathh aassim roozim vananaai

Petitioner do not leave this place empty-handed,
Yes! I do possess some tears,
Take them, should these be of any use to you.
Even after telling everything,
A regret remains,
The only issue I wanted to put across,
Could not be conveyed.

The nineties period constitutes the last phase of Parimu's creative activity even when his hands were weakened by arthritis. His work during this phase shows a sudden transformation from the abstract concretisation to the metaphor of 'Homelessness and Exile' presented through some figurative abstracts.

An expression of pain, suffering, and solidarity with thousands driven out from the peaceful and salubrious environs of the Valley and pushed to the heat and dust of the plains and made to start life from scratch remained his committed engagement during this phase. Some prominent works of this period are:

COBWEBS OF APATHY

If one looks carefully at this work, one finds as if some invisible satanic spider has dragged innocent souls into darkness, hopelessness, misery, isolation, rejection, and apathy. Does it want to trap them permanently? The artist uses faces of simple Kashmiri women with headgear symbolically to pinpoint the victims. Who will free these hapless people from these cobwebs of apathy? Parimu seeks an answer to this question.

SMEARED SNOWS

The work reflects how a beautiful land with hills, snow-clad peaks and silent valleys is engulfed by death and destruction.

RED KNOWS NO CREED

This is a strong voice against the gun culture that knows no caste or creed and is bound to bring pain and suffering for one and all. This painting shows wailing Muslim women from Kashmir who lost their sons, husbands or brothers to the armed militancy in the valley.

Flying Kangri, Exodus I, Exodus II and Charging Rams are some other paintings of this phase. The painting titled Charging Rams represents meek rams trapped and running helter-skelter in panic below the hill. Art critic Suneet Chopra writes in *The Telegraph* newspaper of 4 April 1992:

> One has only to look at his powerful work 'Charging Rams' to see the panic, terror and the anarchy that has been let loose by cynical electoral politicians in his native Kashmir. The luminous red rams breaking through red hot bars give one a powerful impression of what terrorism has done to so many parts of the country today. It also reflects the strange hold of the blind faith and the failure of those who in India were required to educate the masses and make them think beyond the level of a herd of sheep. This particular work is so representative of our contemporary state of affairs that one hopes it will find its place in one of our museums. It is remarkable how all the feelings welling up in Bansi Parimu have burst out in this work.

One of his paintings in the last phase 'The Red Divide' (see page 3) is a powerful portrayal of innocent women trapped in fires and a river of blood. Looking helpless and frightened, the Kashmiri women are shown wearing the traditional Taranga (headgear) and Pheran (cloak).

Bansi Parimu's work adorns most galleries in India and abroad including the prestigious National Gallery of Modern Art, New Delhi, Lalit Kala Akademi, New Delhi, Indian Academy of Fine Arts, Amritsar, the Gallery of Modern Art, Chandigarh, and Contemporary Gallery of Art, Kolkata. His work is also on display inside Delhi College of Art, British Bank of Middle East (Dubai and Kuwait) and the Hearst newspaper office in Cairo. Many foreign diplomatic missions in India have Parimu's paintings on display.

Many private collectors in India and abroad possess Parimu's incredible abstracts. His Green Abstract adorns the walls of the cardiac unit of Nanawati Hospital in Mumbai. His paintings were also used by the UNESCO for their cards. Two of his paintings are prominently displayed at the J&K Governor's house.

The J&K Academy of Art, Culture, and Languages' acquired Parimu's work from time to time. The prominent among these were: Before Deluge (Oil on canvas. Acquired in 1969-70); The Minaret

(Oil on canvas. Acquired in 1970); Pink Setting (Oil on canvas. When acquired not known; Accretion (Oil on canvas. Acquired in 1972); Untitled (Oil on Canvas. Acquired in 1971-72).

Theoretically, the J&K Academy of Art, Culture and Languages should have a rich collection of Parimu's work as the seventies and eighties were its hay days as well as one of the most active periods of Parimu's life as an artist.

Friends from the art fraternity say that not only Bansi Parimu's work but precious works of many national painters are stored in an utterly pitiable condition by the J&K Academy of Art, Culture, and Languages, somewhere, away from the gaze of the public. Capt S K Tikoo says, 'Before marriage, Parimu was careless about earning from the sale of his work. He would spend from his pocket, put his time and energy in his work and then give these paintings free to friends. I was gifted four paintings in that process. They were my prized possessions. Everything was burnt and lost in the blaze as my house was set on fire by miscreants after our migration. I could hardly save anything'.

Some paintings that Bansi Parimu managed to put in his car and take along with him when he left Srinagar are in the custody of his family. How much of his artwork he could bring along in his car is anybody's guesswork. Talking of Parimu's decision to leave Kashmir, Capt S K Tikoo, says:

> What hurt him terribly was when he heard the horrifying slogans in the street: *Aessi chhu banavun Pakistan. Batav ross ta batiniev saan*, meaning, we want our Pakistan, without Pandit men but with Pandit women, *Aey kaafiron aey zaalimon Kashmir hamaara chhorr do*, meaning, O unbeliever! O cruel! Get lost from our Kashmir and *Jisko Kashmir mein rehna hai, Allah-ho-Akbar kehna hai* meaning, anyone who wants to live in Kashmir will have to say Allah-o-Akbar and convert to Islam. One could also see groups of young boys holding Kalashnikov rifles in their hands singing:

Jago! Jago! subah huyee,
Roos ne baazi haari hai ,
Hind pe larza taari hai ,
Ab Kashmir ki baari hai ,
Jago ! Jago ! subah huyee.

Wake up! wake up! It is already dawn ,
Russia has already been defeated.
Now India is under attack
and it is the turn of Kashmir.
Wake up! wake up! It is already dawn.

This environment and the slogans had thrust a dagger into the backbone of the centuries-old composite culture and shared living in the Kashmir valley. And then the gun-wielding and Pakistan-trained militants spared no one who was deemed to be Indian in any manner or who they felt was acting against the objectives of the Azadi movement.

They killed Mushir ul Haq (VC, The University of Kashmir), B K Ganju (engineer employed with BSNL), Sarvanand Koul Premi (poet), Lassa Koul (the then director Doordarshan, Srinagar), Molvi Mohammad Farooq (religious leader), H L Khera (General Manager, HMT, Srinagar), Prem Nath Bhat (advocate), Maulana Masoodi (religious scholar and aged politician), Mustafa Mir (politician) and many government officials and pro-India leaders. These compulsive killers killed people coming out from the mosques after offering prayers. They killed innocent and helpless women and children. They killed innocent people eating food with their family members. Calling them Indian agents, hapless Pandits were used as ducks to test their newly-acquired guns. Innocent men, women, and children were killed. Many women and girls were raped and tortured. I shiver when I recollect those painful memories. And

> for Parimu to leave Kashmir was a very painful decision. I know how bad he felt. He was choked with what was happening in his beloved Kashmir.

Jaya Parimu explains, 'With the closure of schools and colleges in the Kashmir valley, the education of my daughters was badly hit. We left the valley for Jammu to ensure the continuity of the education of our children. We had never thought that we would not return to our house. My husband returned to Srinagar. He still hoped that things would change for the better. But that was not to be so. For days, he could not move out of his house. With no medicines, no petrol in the vehicle and total negativity in the air, he felt choked. Deaths and destruction made him restless. Most of his friends had moved out and there was no social interaction. Close friends suggested to him that he should leave Kashmir because anything could happen anytime. He lived alone with our trusted domestic help. And finally in June 1990, very reluctantly, he moved out. He was pained to see frightened Kashmiri Pandit children and women running for safety in trucks with suitcases and blankets. In Jammu, I asked him, 'what have you brought along with you?' He said, 'I got some essentials, some paintings, and the car. I left all those expensive clothes, pashmina, Persian carpet, and other valuables'. He was depressed and wanted to go back. I had not received my salary. Banks in the Valley were closed. Transferring money from the Valley banks to Jammu was a tough job. Even if you had your money in Srinagar bank, there was no way to draw and use it. 'Did You get your salary?' he asked. I said, 'no'. He had no money. He sold his car in Jammu for twenty thousand rupees. I didn't object. With that cash and our elder daughter Jheelaf, he left for Delhi. He was restless and in a shock.'

Artist Veer Munshi says, 'I came closer to Parimu in Delhi. He had the potential to be a Husain over here, but he did not survive. Had he lived a few years more, he would have dominated the art horizon of the capital and the country. He had the fundamental clarity of concepts. Displacement from the valley had hit his soul. We had one-to-one discussions many times. Tears welled up in his eyes when he talked about what he missed in the heat and dust of the plains'.

Noted actor and theatre director M K Raina recalls:

> A visit to him was a must when I and my wife visited Kashmir. He had a special love for me. He even arranged our stay free of cost once. Many times, he walked with me right from the Palladium cinema up to the India Coffee House and kept talking about his concerns like environment, Dal pollution or extinction of the Chinar tree, etc. And then I saw him in 1990 in Delhi. That time, I found him a changed man. He carried a deep hurt. He felt uprooted like a fish taken out of water. Migration from Kashmir had hit him deep. The scars and the bruises were deep down his soul. This pain was visible in his work too. It probably hastened the process of the degeneration of his body. There were no Coffee House friends. He carried a deep sense of rootlessness. But he carried no ill-feeling against any individual. He nursed the hope of return to his dear Kashmir.

Shantiveer Kaul noted, 'He had artistically built his house. I mean the glass front, the studio, the garden, the flower beds, and all that ambience. I would say that he had put his imagination and blood into it. Living as exile was unbearable for him. He became a victim of many physical ailments. A very tragic end of a dear friend. It took me some time to reconcile to the reality of his not being around'.

Senior Journalist Rahul Jalali reminisces, 'I knew him very well. He was close to my father too. I remember his *Grih pravesh* (house warming) after he constructed his new house at Barzulla in Srinagar. He was proud of his house and told us that he had designed it, especially the attic. The attic had a huge window facing the Zabarwan hills. That was the room where he painted. In 2015, I visited Barzulla and tried to locate his house, but could not. Later, someone told me that it had been pulled down and a new building had been constructed at the

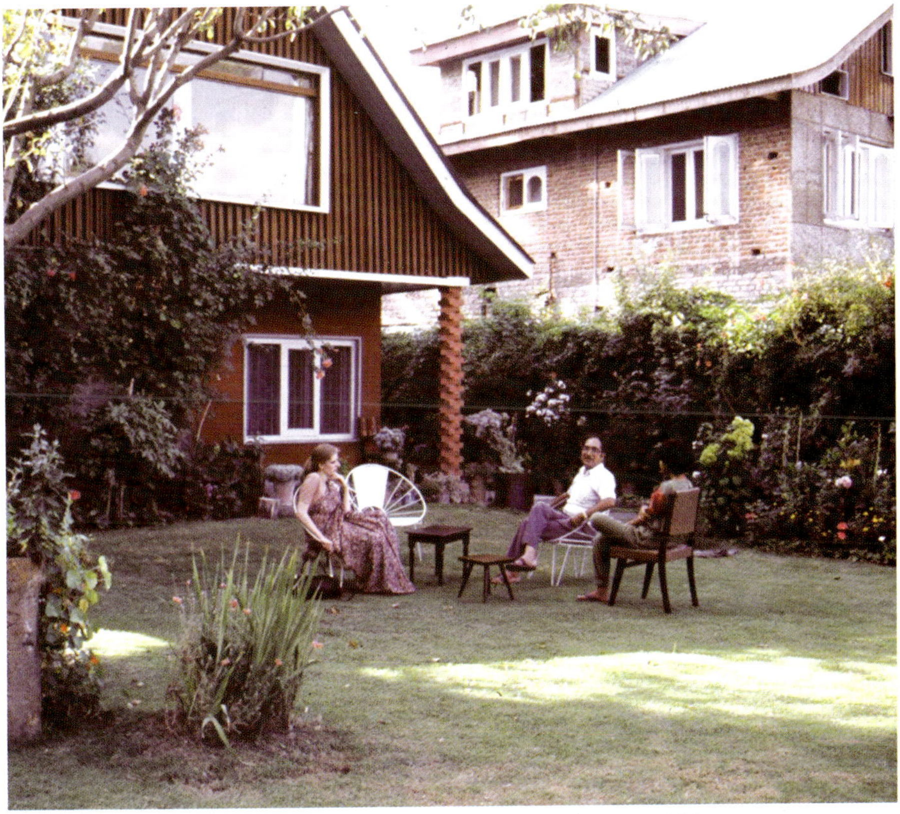

Bansi Parimu in his Srinagar house Takhleeq

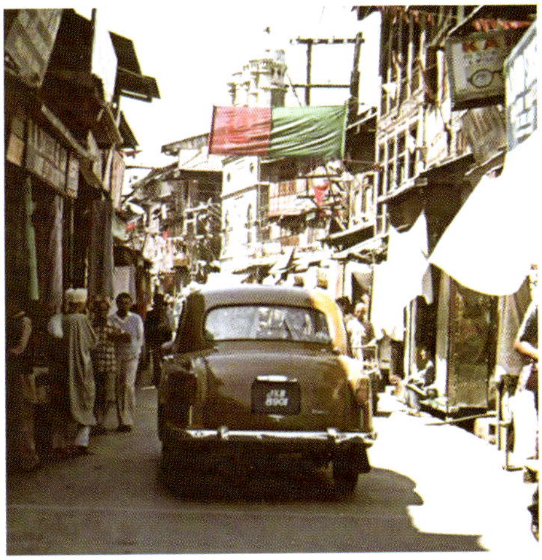

The road outside Bansi Parimu's old house at Habba Kadal

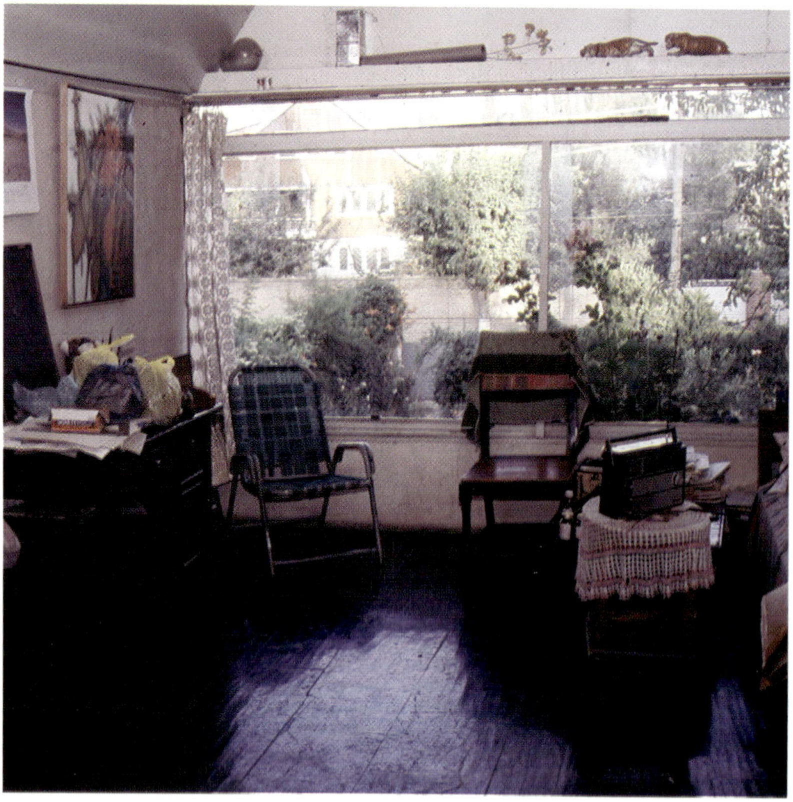

The view from Studio of Bansi Parimu's Barzulla house

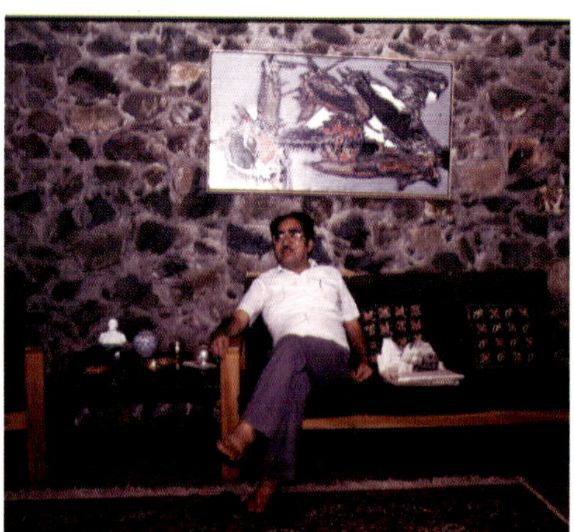

Bansi Parimu in his Barzulla house

spot. That house symbolises what Kashmir is today. All the things of beauty have been pulled down'.

In Delhi, he had to start from scratch. He had never lived in the hot and humid climate of the plains. He had to run for so many issues in the scorching heat or choking humidity. He arranged the college admission of his daughter. Besides, he set up a house in Ghaziabad and created a mini studio for himself.

He built a new circle of friends, many fellow sufferers, and met frequently at Coffee House, Connaught Place. He painted at night and wrote for newspapers in the day. He gave vent to his feelings through interviews to newspaper such as *The Hindu* and the *Times of India.* Delhi was politically vibrant and alive. He joined SAHMAT rallies against communalism. In spite of losing everything, he never lost his objectivity and clarity.

In a *Times of India* Interview that he gave to Shamsul Islam, published on 4 August 1991, he said, 'I am yet to settle down in Delhi. Most of my time is consumed in running from one place to another for ration card, gas, and admission of my daughter to a college. Rules don't mention that migrants will arrive from Kashmir, so the bureaucracy is insensitive'.

Ropal kohan Kalas taaj
Karaan yaarie panun raaj
*Raesseul *Vehak turun* Maagh*
Natchaan vigieni gyavaan raag
Vasaan shraani chhalaan daagh
Panun bagh matchueil bagh
Hutyein boeni Yetyein naag
Panun bagh matchueil bagh

Snow-capped silvery peaks,
like crowns on mountain heads.
And over these mountains,

pine trees holding their own kingdom.
A pleasurable Vaisakha![1]
A cold Maaga![2]
A heavy downpour,
meant to wash away all our wounds,
dancing fairies
singing melodious Ragas,
that is my garden,
my love-filled garden,
endowed with Chinar trees
and freshwater springs.
That is my garden,
my love-filled garden.
—Moti Lal Saqi

These lines from Moti Lal Saqi's poem define what Kashmir meant to Bansi Parimu. For him, snow-capped peaks, dense forests, lofty Chinars, colourful flowers, happy birds, freshwater springs, gardens and above all the age-old coexistence and pluralism all put together was Kashmir. Never ever in his wildest dreams could he think of parting from this Kashmir that he loved intensely. But it was not to be so.

1 Kashmir has six seasons, each of two months duration. These can be summed up as:-

1. Spring - From March 15 to May 15. Known as Soant in Kashmiri
2. Summer - From May 15 to July 15. Known as Greeshim in Kashmiri
3. Rainy Season - From July 15 to Sept. 15. Known as Vaharaat in Kashmiri
4. Autumn - From Sept. 15 to Nov. 15. Known as Harud in Kashmiri
5. Winter - From Nov. 15 to Jan 15. Known as Vandha in Kashmiri
6. Ice cold - From Jan. 15 to March 15. Known as Shishur in Kashmiri

The calendar followed by Kashmiri Pandits has following months:-
Chaitra, Vaisakh, Jyeshtha, Ashadh, Shravan, Bhadra, Ashwin, Kartik, Marg, Paush, Magh, Falgun. In Kashmiri, these months are known as... Tsitter, Vehak, Zeth, Haar, Shravun, Ba'drepeth, A'shid, Kartik, Monjhor, Poh, Maagh and Faagun.

2 ibid

CONNECTING KASHMIR TO THE WIDER WORLD OF ART

Bansi Parimu's role in facilitating and helping the J&K Academy of Art, Culture, and Languages to host and organise art camps and workshops is no less a contribution. He wished to familiarise local artists with current styles and trends in modern art. Most of the Mumbai or Delhi based artists were personally known to him. Quite often, it was through his support, good offices and help that the J&K Academy of Art, Culture, and Languages was in a position to bring many leading artists of the country to various art camps in the State. These camps were attended by a galaxy of eminent artists like N S Bendre, Jagdish Swaminathan, B C Sanyal, Rameshwar Broota, Kashmiri Khosa, Shamshad Hussain, Shanko Choudhry, S H Raza, Gulam Sheikh, M F Husain, Ram Kumar, G R Santosh, Manu Parikh, Paramjit Singh, Jatin Dass and many others.

Noted art critic, Santo Datta, writes in *The Hindu* newspaper of 3 August 1992:

> One of Parimu's memorable contributions is the initiation of an ongoing programme of holding annual artists' camps in Srinagar, in which artists were invited from all parts of the country. His objective was to start interaction between the artists of Kashmir and those from other States.

Sculptor Rajendra Tiku recalls, 'Parimu had a great desire to introduce modern trends to local artists by simple interactions. Husain was quite friendly with him. I have seen them together many times in Srinagar at the fashionable Residency Road or in the India Coffee House. I vividly remember how he brought M F Husain to the Institute of Music and Fine Arts, Srinagar for a live demonstration. Many students were benefited by observing Husain doing live painting and then interacting with him.'

Shantiveer Kaul points out, 'Bansiji was a bridge between artists at the national scene and artists from the State. The art camps in Kashmir were a result of his initiative. I attended the Ganderbal art camp. It was a wonderful and eventful occasion with many national artists participating. It would have been impossible to hold these camps had he not involved himself'. The encouragement to art and artistic activity was brought down to the district level from the Srinagar city by artists and connoisseurs of art. Bansi Parimu played a key role in this diffusion of art to rural Kashmir.'

Trade union leader Indu Bhushan Zutshi recalls:

> In the early seventies, an association of artists was formed in Anantnaag. This association had some prominent artists of the Anantnaag district as its members. Artists like Makhan Lal Goja, Shafi Chaman, Vijay Zutshi, Sham Lal Khaar, Neeraj Bakshi and Bansi Tikoo held regular exhibitions in the district to promote art. One such exhibition was attended by Bansi Parimu. Parimu had brought M Y Taing, the then Secretary, J&K Academy of Art, Culture, and Languages along with him. Another exhibition was attended by Prof Hajini and the noted Kashmiri poet, Arjun Dev Majboor. These exhibitions were seen by college and school students apart from the public in general. Bansi Parimu was the main motivator in organising such exhibitions.

So, who was this Bansi Parimu, who spread art to every nook and corner of Kashmir and thought of himself as the voice of Kashmir outside the State – rooted in the soil, the son who took Kashmir's art and politics out of its regional confines – the one who was close friends with some of the biggest names in the world of art like Raza, Souza, Husain and acted as a bridge in bringing the world of art in India to Srinagar? To know this, we have to return to the world of art and politics in Kashmir at the time of Bansi's birth, the milieu he came from and the renaissance that happened post-freedom of the country in the first half of the twentieth century.

As an artist, he could have earned more name and fame had he come out of the Kashmir valley and moved to a metropolitan city. He did move to New Delhi in the last year of his life, but it was under constrained circumstances. He left his home, friends, and his beloved Kashmir when armed militancy arrived in that part of the country. As an exile in New Delhi, his health deteriorated fast and he left this world forever when he was barely 58 years old. He left many dreams and projects incomplete. He had a stream of admirers both within and outside Kashmir. His work decorates many galleries within the country and outside. The human being in him always remained taller than the artist that he was.

THE EARLY YEARS

Jo rukay to koh-e-garaan thay hum,
jo chalay to jaan se guzar gaye
Rah-e-yaar hum ne qadam qadam,
tujhay yaadgaar banaa diya....

For when we stayed, we rose like massifs,
and when we strayed, we left life far behind;
fellow-traveller, every step that we ever took
became a memorial to your life.
—Faiz Ahmed Faiz

AFTER 1947, THE art scenario in Kashmir was not only reactivated but it changed altogether for the better. Apart from going to Baroda, Mumbai, Delhi and later getting training at the Institute of Music and Fine Arts in Srinagar, a few aspiring artists worked on their own simply by watching or observing the paintings of old masters, attending workshops and art exhibitions and by remaining in touch with established artists in and outside the Kashmir valley. One such person who did it on his own was Bansi Lal Sapru, who later came to be known as Bansi Parimu.

The Saprus are well known Saraswat Brahmins from Kashmir. This surname brings to mind some well-known personalities in the subcontinent such as Tej Bahadur Sapru (freedom fighter and reputed lawyer), Allama Iqbal[1] (from a Sapru Brahmin family that had embraced Islam), Justice P N Sapru (judge Allahabad High Court and Rajya Sabha member), T N Sapru (eminent authority on jurisprudence and noted author), D K Sapru (well-known cinema actor), Tej Sapru (cinema actor) and Jagdish Narain Sapru (former chairman ITC). Sapru Brahmins are descendants of Rishi Aupamanyava, a sage of the ancient Vedic period. For this reason, the Gotra[2] of Sapru Brahmins from Kashmir is *'Dipat Saman Aupamanyava'*.

It is believed that the Saprus originally belonged to the village Saprein near Kulgam town in south Kashmir. From Kulgam, they moved to different places in Kashmir valley for many reasons, essentially economic. In Srinagar city, Saprus mostly lived around the Habba Kadal locality. It is believed that Saprus of Sapriyaar, Habba Kadal had come to live in this locality much before the Afghan rule in Kashmir. And Pandit Madhav Lal Sapru from this Sapriyaar clan of Saprus adopted a boy from the Raina family of Kandi Khas, Handwara (north Kashmir). The boy was named Gopi Nath, and came to be known as Gopi Nath Sapru. Gopi Nath Sapru was married at a very young age. He had seven children from this marriage: three daughters and four sons. One male child, born on 2 June 1933, was named Bansi Lal.

---

1 Allama Iqbal's ancestors were undoubtedly Sapru Brahmin from Kashmir. All along his life, he remained warm towards Kashmiri Brahmins . In *Javednama*, Allama writes:-

"A'an brahman zaadganan-e-zindah dil
Laleh-e-ahmar zi rooye sha'n khajil
Tez been-o-pukhta kaar-o- sakht kosh
Az nigah-e-sha'n farang andar kharosh
Asl-e-sha'n az khaake-e-daamangeer ma'st,
Matla-e-ein akhtara'n Kashmir ma'st "

Those scions of Brahmans with vibrant hearts,
their glowing cheeks put the red tulip to shame.
Keen of eye, mature and strenuous in action,
their very glance puts Europe into commotion.
Their origin is from this protesting soil of ours,
the rising place of these stars is our Kashmir.

2 The Gotra is a system which associates a person with his most ancient or root ancestor in an unbroken male lineage.

Madhav Lal Sapru had a daughter who was married in the Parimu family of Srinagar but unfortunately, she became a widow at a very young age. Her in-laws were not in good terms with this young widow and, accordingly, she was brought back to her parental home where she lived in the joint family.

To keep her busy and engaged, Madhav Lal suggested to his daughter that she should adopt Gopi Nath Sapru's son Bansi Lal to which she readily agreed. That day onwards, Bansi Lal Raina-Sapru became Bansi Lal Parimu or Bansi Parimu without any change in the residential location or family house.

WHO ARE PARIMUS?

One Sukh Ram Razdan had returned to Kashmir sometime around 1770 CE, after living in the plains of the country. The members of the orthodox Kashmiri Pandit community, who had stayed back in Kashmir during the dark Afghan rule, nicknamed him Sukh Ram Aparium (outsider). Subsequently, his son, Ram Joo Razdan was named as Ram Joo Parium. Parium is an abbreviation of Aparium. Finally, Parium became Parimu.

CHILDHOOD

The young boy Bansi Lal, though adopted by his father's widowed sister, remained deeply attached to his biological mother whom he fondly called Dhanna (Dhanwati). Dhanwati died when Bansi Lal was barely ten years of age. That was possibly the first emotional setback and shock to the sensitive child.

Bansi Lal used to slip out of the house and watch a tonga (horse cart) moving on the road outside the family's old house at Habba Kadal. Quite often, he would sit on the banks of the Jhelum River near the Purshyaar temple, and watch the river flow. Sometimes, he was seen watching the birds in the sky and the people walking over the Habba Kadal bridge.

As Bansi Lal opened his eyes to the world, he saw poverty all around him. He saw that his family had just one breadwinner and many mouths to feed. For many days, the family had to live by eating boiled potatoes as grains or pulses were simply beyond their reach. ML Sapru, Bansi Lal's elder brother, was studying for his graduation and also carried tiffin for one of the employees of Amresh Talkies, a local movie hall, for which he was paid rupees three per month. The lack of resources and appalling poverty made young Bansi Lal a rebel and agnostic. It may be relevant to mention that Amresh Talkies[3] at Regal Chowk, Srinagar was owned by the Bals, a Punjabi Khatri family of Kashmir.

Bansi Lal was sent to school, where he took more interest in extracurricular activities than studies. He loved his drawing classes the most. During his stay at the school, he remained a monitor and leader solely because of his active participation in extracurricular activities. The Germany-based historian and writer, Peter (Predimen Krishen) Raina, and theatre stalwart Moti Lal Kemu, were his close friends in National School, Srinagar. Talking of Raina, Jaya Parimu, says, 'Peter or Predimen Krishen Raina is the son of Pandit Jia Lal Raina Taarivol, a very senior revenue official from Kashmir. Peter was Parimu's childhood friend. He was thrilled to see Parimu married and settled in his own house at Barzulla in Kashmir. He came over

3 One philanthropic Sikh gentleman, Bhai Anant Singh Gauri brought cinema to the Kashmir valley by opening the Palladium Talkies at Lal Chowk, Srinagar sometime in 1932. Ardeshir Irani's *Alam-Ara* was the first movie screened in this hall. When the Sher-e-Kashmir Institute of Medical Sciences was set up at Soura (Srinagar), Bhai Anant Singh donated more than 50 Kanals of land for this premier medical centre in the Kashmir valley. Bhai Anant Singh kept his cinema hall at the disposal of the National Militia or Peace Brigade cadres of Kashmir after the tribal raid of 1947. During that period, the cinema hall also became the headquarter of the emergency administration headed by Sheikh Mohammed Abdullah. The Palladium was followed by the Regal cinema owned by the Bals.
The Bal family had a cinema hall in Lahore as well. They had another cinema at Gulmarg that remained closed during winters. Later, this family opened one more cinema hall near Regal cinema in Srinagar, known as Amresh Talkies. The Bal siblings — Amresh Bal, Prakash Bal and Mahinder Bal did cinema business in Lahore and Kashmir through a firm known as Universal Pictures Limited. The Bal family had a bungalow at Gupkar Road in Srinagar and another house at Raj Bagh, apart from other properties in the Kashmir valley. In 1950, both Regal and Amresh cinemas were sold to Bakshi Abdul Majid, brother of Bakshi Ghulam Mohammad by the Bals. Both the cinema halls were set ablaze on 28 December 1963 by an infuriated mob protesting against the mysterious disappearance of the holy relic from the Hazrat Bal shrine in Srinagar. World-renowned fashion designer, Rohit Bal is from this Bal family of Kashmir.

with my brother and Bhabhi to our house. He liked the small house, and told me that Parimu, like a leader, would go up a mound of earth in the school and give lectures at the age of nine or ten. He also said Parimu would make posters and charts for the classrooms using natural colours obtained from tree leaves, clay, and bricks'.

Peter Raina (born 1935) is an internationally acclaimed writer who has authored about 20 books on Polish history, the anti-communist movement, Polish church and politics in Polish, a language that he mastered. While In Poland, he joined a group of free thinkers who were opposed to the curbs and restrictions imposed during the communist rule. Like other Polish intellectuals who opposed the communist dictatorship in Poland, he was banished from Poland where he had been permanently living since 1962. In Poland, his close friends included reputed writers like Mieczyslaw Jastrun and Pawel Jasienic and the national icon of the Polish church, Bishop Wyszynski. Finally, Peter Raina moved to Germany as an exile and taught at the Berlin University. In Poland, Peter Raina fell in love with a Polish girl, Barbara Wyreszczynska, a pretty, blonde student at Warsaw University and married her in 1968. They were a wonderful couple. This marriage had a tragic end. A documentary on Peter Raina by Bozena Garus-Hockuba, a Polish filmmaker, makes us believe that his wife was possibly killed by Służba Bezpieczeństwa, the secret police of the then communist government of Poland. Peter Raina's contribution to Polish life and democracy will go down in the annals of Polish history as extraordinary.

Like his friend, Parimu too was a socialist to the core. Capt S K Tikoo, Bansi Parimu's lifelong friend, recalls, 'In National School, he was senior to me. Every year, we juniors bade farewell to 10th class students by organising a grand event and singing *Alvida Alvida*. He led that event once and I remember his meticulous involvement for that event. It was 1945 or 1946. During his school days, he was more drawn towards drawing and model-making than books'.

Bansi must have been barely ten when winds of historic changes swept the subcontinent. On the national stage, Gandhi was impelling Indians to launch a nationwide non-violent movement to protest against the unjust laws and acts implemented by the British. In his homeland, a kingdom, clouds of resentment had begun to gather. Sheikh Mohammad Abdullah led the movement against the Maharaja's rule, poverty, and exploitation. The Communist movement had also gained a foothold in India and some communist leaders considered Kashmir as a laboratory for testing the communist way of life. In the early 1940s, communism crossed the Pir Panjal mountains and arrived in the Kashmir valley.

As a young boy, Bansi Parimu felt that this new belief was a panacea for many social ills and inequalities in his homeland. He saw people like M L Misri, D P Dhar, G M Sadiq, N N Raina, Peer Gias-ud-Din, Pran Nath Jalali, and Dina Nath Nadim adopt this socio-political ideology. He and many young men saw communism as a new hope for deliverance against miseries and poverty. This was the basis of Parimu's fundamental belief in the communist ideology. When I interviewed his friends and relations in 2017 and 2018 for this book, it became quite clear that his belief in communism was not bookish. He was conscious of the social realities around him.

At a very young age, he had developed a total disregard for religious rituals. But he maintained his belief in spirituality. He used to tell his friends: 'Religion may divide because it does not tolerate questioning. Spirituality is a search for the real truth. It is thus a great effort towards unity.'

Hriday Nath Jattu, a Kashmiri Pandit leader, points out, 'Bansi Parimu had a communist bent of mind. But I have seen him as a man who believed in some sort of spirituality and Kashmir's sainthood. From him, I also secured some donations for a social cause.'

Having focused on drawing and model-making in school, young Bansi Lal saw a new art movement taking birth in Kashmir. The renewed interest in art was created by a group of educated artists led by Triloke Kaul, P N Kachru and S N Butt. Well-known artist S H Raza's visit to Srinagar had given a sudden momentum to this movement. The interest in art and painting at that point in the Kashmir valley was something unusual and unheard of. Drawing or art was at the most considered a hobby, and not a career option for young boys and girls at that time.

ON THE BANKS OF THE JHELUM

THE CORE GROUP of Kashmiri artists lived from Badiyar to Fateh Kadal on either side of the Jhelum river in Srinagar city. The artists Shiv Nath Raina, Mohan Raina, Ratan Parimoo, S N Butt, D N Walli, Kishori Kaul, Triloke Kaul, Som Nath Khosa, Suraj Tiku, Kashi Nath Bhan, A R John, G R Santosh, Maheshwar Nath Dhar, Sant Ji Sultan, J N Sapru, Shuben Kaw, Nissar Aziz, Mohi-ud-Din, Vishinath Kampasi, Sat Lal Kampasi and many more lived in this area. And Bansi Parimu lived in close proximity to all of them, in a locality known as Sapriyaar near Habba Kadal Bridge.

Where to go and how to learn? That was the issue for young Bansi. He kept visiting any and every place where he could pick up something about art. Pandit Shiv Nath Raina (1901-1961) was his first teacher. Shiv Nath Raina lived at Badiyar Bala and was trained at Sir Amar Singh Technical Institute, Srinagar by renowned instructors like Fred Andrews and J C Mukerjee. Shiv Nath imparted free training in the use of paint and watercolours to many aspiring artists. Among those who visited Shiv Nath Raina to learn art included G R Santosh, S N Butt, Suraj Tiku and Amar Nath Vaishnavi (social worker and a leader of the Kashmiri Pandits) and many others.

Apart from Shiv Nath Raina, Dwarka Nath Gigoo 'Rajkamal' and D N Walli (1908-2006) were Parimu's initial teachers. He would sit with them and watch them paint. Dwarka Nath Gigoo Rajkamal lived at Khankaah-e-Sokhta in downtown Srinagar. He had varied interests like painting, music (he played flute and banjo), astrology, palmistry, and poetry. Since Gigoo was not concentrating on painting alone, Bansi Parimu started frequenting D N Walli's house. He lived at Badiyar Bala in Srinagar city. Walli too had got his training at Sir Amar Singh Technical Institute and later in Kolkata. Using watercolours as his medium, Kashmir was visible everywhere in his work. His special focus was to present speaking images of life in Kashmir. He painted women engaged in daily chores, children, boatmen, fisherwomen, Bazars, snow landscapes, autumn Chinars, poplars, rice husking activity, hills, streams, animals, birds, river Ghats, temples, mosques, canals, fruit-laden trees and houses with thatched roofs. He also painted the innocence and the poverty of the people of his native land, Kashmir.

When we look at Walli's work, we don't need to read much to know how people lived in Kashmir six or seven decades ago. Every frame conveys how Kashmiris lived in their not-so-distant past. He would book a Shikara and carry his watercolours for sale to the tourists living in the houseboats. Walli was fully aware of various forms of modern art, especially cubism and impressionism but he focused on Kashmir's landscapes alone. The progressive group of artists consisting of Triloke Koul, P N Kachru, S N Butt and even Ghulam Rasool Santosh tried hard to bring this stalwart to the modern art camp but failed. He remained steadfast to his medium, style, and subject. Walli was a major attraction for Bansi Parimu during his formative years. Observing Walli doing watercolours, Bansi learned the fundamentals of watercolour painting. And he began his artistic journey with landscapes done in watercolours.

Walli's son, T K Walli, recalls: 'My father, whom we fondly called Babuji, was deeply inspired by Van Gogh after he read the biographical account of the painter in the book, *Lust for Life*. He was equally influenced by great masters of the renaissance period like Goya and Rembrandt, especially the latter's Night Watchman, which displays a wonderful balance of light and shade in the picture.

Babuji had a strong belief in God's existence. To us, he would often recite verses composed by Lal Ded and Nund Reshi. I also remember our parents visiting Sufi saint Sona Sahib, living in the village called Darvesh Gaam, in the Anantnag area. There we listened to verses from the Holy Quran and Shlokas from Bhagavad Gita. In spite of knowing all modern trends, he never deviated from his passion for painting Kashmir and its beauty. He never changed his style and subject. Percy Brown, Sardar K M Pannikar, S K Patil, O C Ganguli, M S Randhawa and Keshav Malik were admirers of his subject and style.'

Besides Walli, Bansi Parimu would also visit S N Butt where he got exposed to French impressionism, cubism, and other modern trends and styles. Butt had been influenced by Picasso, George Braque, Vincent Van Gogh, Degas, and Renoir. He had seen their work sometime in 1942, when he went to Mumbai for training in modern art under the well-known artist, G M Salgaonkar. Butt had also been trained by Raza in modern art styles. Raza had gifted some books to Butt that had paintings of Vincent Van Gogh and many other modern artists. Parimu found Butt's work of great interest. Marxism was also a common cord that kept Bansi tied to Butt. Like all progressives of his time, Butt too had Marxist leanings. He had seen pain, suffering, and poverty. In October 1947, he too volunteered to serve the refugees from Baramulla town who had been housed in many school buildings of Srinagar city after the tribal raid. The pain and suffering that he witnessed in these school camps pushed him more towards the communist ideology, but he did not join any political party.

Ramesh Kumar Butt, son of artist Som Nath Butt, recalls: 'My father sang K L Saigal's songs. Dilip Kumar was his favourite actor. He saw Dilip Kumar's Daag thirty times. He was greatly touched by Dilip Kumar's role as Devdas. Poet Dina Nath Nadim was a frequent visitor to our house. My father had designed the sets for Nadim Sahib's opera, Bombur-Yemberzal. He enjoyed Sufiana music, Lal Vaakhs, and Shams Faqir's compositions. He always kept a photograph of Swami Ram Tirath in his pocket. My sisters, Asha and Veena, were quite attached to him. He appeared to be a Marxist but at heart, he was a Dervish (saint) in the real sense. He was full of compassion and yet careless about his own self. He gifted many priceless paintings to his friends. He would easily believe anyone and was moved by pain and suffering.'

During my research work for this book, I came to know four of Butt's paintings, titled 'The Houses', 'Landscape-I', 'Landscape-II' and 'Autumn', were acquired by the J&K Academy of Art, Culture, and Languages before his death but the fate of these paintings is not known. I also learnt that Butt had attended the October 1949 exhibition held by the Progressive Artists Association in New Delhi.

This was the first major art exhibition held by the Progressive Artists Association outside the State and was widely covered by newspapers. The newspapers described S N Butt as a 'wizard of colour combinations'. I also came to know that a watercolour portrait of Som Nath Butt done by Raza in 1948 was sold by a Mumbai art auctioneer in June 2018 for USD 19,800 (About 13.06 lakh rupees). Jaya Parimu recalls: 'During his formative years, Parimu was highly influenced by Som Nath Butt. Butt's main forte was figurative abstracts, homes, roofs, attics, etc. He was one of twentieth century's great artist. He had received praise from the British art connoisseurs. Alcohol spoiled his health and family life. He died unsung and now remains unheard of in the world of art.'

Bansi Parimu was also a frequent visitor to Kashi Nath Bhan's house. Kashi Nath Bhan was a multi-talented person from Kashmir who had been a teacher at the Sir Amar Singh Technical Institute in Srinagar. Later, he joined the Industrial Training Institute at Bagh-e-Dilawar Khan in Srinagar as an art teacher. Kashi Nath Bhan was a much-respected name in the field of theatre and fine arts and his students included prominent artists like Mohammad Sadiq and Nisar Aziz Beg.

The son of artist Suraj Tiku, Santosh Tiku, remembers: 'Bansi Parimu would come to our house regularly. My father was a trained artist and a little older than him. Parimu and my father held long discussions on the trends and styles in art. Sometimes, these discussions were also on the use of colours and mediums for painting. Parimu had already established himself as an artist in the valley. He also sought suggestions from my father. Both of them held Kashi Nath Bhan in high esteem.'

Talking about Bansi Parimu's formative years and struggle, author Arvind Gigoo says:

> Apart from Kishori Kaul, Santji Sultan, and Nisar Aziz Beg, Bansi Parimu was another regular visitor to our house. He used to see my uncle Dwarka Nath Gigoo Rajkamal often. My uncle was a writer, painter, flautist, palmist, and astrologer. I have seen young Bansi draw sketches in the presence of my uncle. One day, Bansiji asked me to draw some random lines on a sheet of paper. I drew the lines and handed over the paper sheet to him. He joined all the lines and to my surprise, I saw the sketches of a man, a woman, and a building. It was sheer magic. That day I understood his artistic originality and prowess. And one day we went together to see the film, *Do Ankhein Baraah Haath*. By together I mean myself, Bansiji, my uncle, and Santji Sultan. We walked on the road singing, *Aey maalik tere bande hum*.
>
> I have been to his somewhat decrepit house at Habba Kadal. He had a small room where he would paint, make models or write. He had made a model from a soap bar. He had bought two slabs of homemade soap and carved a crescent, a star and a lotus by the careful use of a knife. He displayed that model to the public outside his house. Many people visited his house to see these beautiful and unusual models. A Muslim visitor said, 'Bansiji, you have made crescent and a star. May Allah grant you good health and luck'. Pandit visitors would say, 'He has made Brahma's lotus. May he prosper!'.
>
> As he grew, he picked up trends and styles. I could see how perfect and swiftly his fingers moved. This was something gifted

> and natural. Bansiji always kept close association with people connected with art.
>
> This appetite drew him closer to some leading artists of the State. Later it brought him closer to some renowned artists of the country. His observation was sharp. He was an inquisitive man who had an incredible appetite for learning, assimilation, and experimentation. He learned by observation and scrutiny. He believed in painting, tearing apart the art paper, painting again and again till he was satisfied. He was a perfectionist. He thus practised the centuries-old Vedic doctrine of *Neti Neti*. It was a process of self-learning or an appraisal of reality through self-inquiry and investigation.

In *Miraas* (January–June 2019 issue), Jaya Parimu's nephew Vijay Vishen writes:

> Once I showed him (Bansi Parimu) a few pebbles picked up by me from Lidder stream at Pahalgam in Kashmir. He took a large and irregular stone from the collection and in a few minutes transformed it into a beautiful paperweight with a symbolic 'foot and flower' painted on it.
>
> The paperweight remains one of my prized possessions. On another occasion, the two of us were on a project to make a unique piece of furniture – a tripod with legs made out of the branches from the mulberry tree in the kitchen garden, with the bark intact, and the top flat piece from a walnut tree irregular in shape. The table, artistically done, was put by him in his living room and it struck the eye of one and all visiting his house, Takhleeq.

Well-known media personality, writer and broadcaster, Pran Kishore Kaul, recollects an anecdote relating to Bansi Parimu's first meeting with the progressives.

> I too was initially inclined towards art. The progressive group

comprising Triloke Kaul, S N Butt and P N Kachru would meet every Friday at a restaurant on the Bund. This restaurant was owned by Mr Madan, an educated entrepreneur who was also a connoisseur of art. One Friday, possibly in 1954, two young boys also joined us. One was Bansi Lal Parimu, and the other was Mohan Lal Moza. Bansi had brought some paintings along with him. Incidentally, G R Santosh had also come that day. This young boy, who later came to be known as Bansi Parimu, had a passion and was different. He was experimenting, and everyone including S N Butt felt happy to see his work. That is my first memory of seeing Bansi Parimu. Later, I kept watching this young boy and his work. His drawing turned robust. He attained an individual style of colour application. These colours were vibrant and attracted attention. He arrived at the pure abstract format after having meandered through landscapes, cubism, and figurative abstracts. He also did some larger works like tableaus.

About Bansi Parimu's joining the 'National Cultural Front' (National Cultural Congress) in Kashmir, Pran Kishore Kaul writes this:-

> S N Butt and Triloke Kaul would sometimes drop in but never became members of the National Cultural Front. Nor would G R Santosh get affiliated to it. But they too were busy on their own and had followed the line of the Progressive Artists Group of Bombay and had organised themselves under the banner of 'Progressive Artists Association'. 'The National Cultural Front' was re-christened the 'National Cultural Congress' in October 1949. Besides S N Butt, Triloke Kaul, P N Kachru and G R Santosh, there were a few beginners like me who became the members of the Cultural Front. These were Bansi Parimu, Nisar Aziz, Mohan Lal Moza, Umesh Kaul and a couple of others whose names I do not remember now as most of them drifted away after some time. This was perhaps the most important

> phase of the development or modern art in Kashmir. S N Butt was the guiding force and we all held him in high respect in spite of the fact that we did not have big age difference.

'Bansi Parimu soon became a member of National Cultural Congress. This was perhaps the most important phase of the development of modern art in Kashmir. Butt was the guiding force and we all held him in high esteem,' added Pran Kishore Kaul.

In 2017, during my visit to the US, I happened to meet Muneebur Rehman, the son of the well-known Kashmiri poet and writer Amin Kamil. Working at the Boston Institute of Languages and also editing a Kashmiri literary journal, NEAB (started by his father in Kashmir) in the US, Muneebur Rehman recalled that Bansi Parimu was a friend of his father, Kashmiri writer Hriday Kaul Bharti and his brother Umesh Kaul. In 2019, I talked to Hriday Kaul Bharti. He was kind enough to agree to a telephonic interview in spite of being unwell. He said:

> Bansi was a frequent visitor to our house. He was a bosom friend of my elder brother, Umesh. Our entire family treated him as a son born to my mother. He was always restless and in a great hurry. Poverty had played an unpleasant role in his life during childhood and early youth. He had set up his studio at Habba Kadal that he named, Prerna Studio. He had learnt the basics of photography and portraiture from the only Studio at Kharyar, Habba Kadal those days. He visited SN Butt's house regularly with my elder brother Umesh. Umesh and Bansi watched Butt work on his canvases and later both of them recreated similar work at their own places. My brother learned art only because of his association with SN Butt. And Butt had also been exposed by Raza to some forms of modern art.
>
> Those days people would not go for camera photographs for many reasons. In the Kashmiri Pandit families, one saw painted portraits of the elders who were no more around. Bansi Parimu made many such portraits at his Prerna Studio. He would also

paint Hindu gods and deities. His younger brother, who later worked for the J&K Police, joined me at Prem Sangeet Niketan for some time but left halfway. Bansi was persuaded to complete his B A degree course via a shortcut, after clearing Prabhakar and some other Hindi examination as a private student. He joined coaching classes for this degree but left halfway due to financial constraints. I could feel and see that Bansi needed to earn money.

Bansi once narrated an interesting anecdote to me about his struggle. He told me that for two successive seasons, he went to Punjab to earn money by painting images in fairs. In one such fair, a lady told him in chaste Punjabi, *'Mainu kaanha bana dhe'* or paint Kaanha for me. Bansi did not know the meaning of the word 'Kaanha'. So he asked the lady. And upon coming to know that 'Kaanha' meant Sri Krishna, he drew Sri Krishna's image in no time. The lady took the picture and paid him some money and left. To Bansi Parimu's surprise, she returned hurriedly and said, *'Aey ki banaaya. Maakhanchor di looli te banaai nee'* meaning, What have you made? You have not drawn baby Sri Krishna's sex organ. And Bansi Parimu had to ask a Sikh gentleman what *'Looli'* meant. Thereafter, he drew many images of Sri Krishna. He began his work by drawing baby Sri Krishna's looli first. That was a period of his desperate struggle to earn something for the family. Then came a time when he worked hard on anything that came his way. He dabbled in political activity without any personal goals. For some period, he became a kingmaker. His sincerity and desire to learn from any source made him an affectionate friend of some doyens of art on the national scene of the country. They noticed his zeal, dash, and finesse that he had finally picked up. He was an activist of so many genuine causes. I give all credit to him for his success. It was simply a result of his hard work, compassionate nature and integrity. I also remember that he worked as an ace photographer and correspondent of

> the English weekly, Criterion. He had an unmatched mind to pick up anything by simple observation. His anger softened after marriage.

Due to his political activism, Bansi Parimu had attracted the attention of everybody in the administration. His posters, banners and dedicated social work were noticed by all in the political hierarchy that belonged to the educated class. Men like G M Sadiq, D P Dhar, Syed Mir Qasim, Peer Gias-ud-din and many others not only appreciated art but respected artists.

Noted artist Triloke Kaul, while acknowledging Parimu's artistic sensibilities, says: 'Bansiji belonged to a generation that followed us. He was self-taught and prolific in that generation. P N Kachru asked me to see his work. We were always busy with the office work and there were no telephones or mobile phones in those days. One day I saw what he had painted. The paintings were impressive. I found him restless and eager to make it on his own. That is the mark of genuine creativity. He should have lived to flourish.'

Makhan Lal Saraf, the doyen of the theatre movement in J&K recalls:

> Bakshi Sahib's *Jashn-e-Kashmir* of 1956 opened many opportunities for artists, writers, and other creative people. It brought many creative people into limelight and Bansi Parimu was one among them. After Jashn-e-Kashmir, the State Information Department (J&K) started engaging artists for making posters, creating murals for exhibitions and preparing publicity material. I have seen him learning from Kashi Nath Bhan, D N Walli, and S N Butt. He was more drawn towards Butt during his formative years. He would also read a lot of literature. Sadiq Sahib was a real connoisseur of art. He held Bansi Parimu In high esteem. Because of his talent, Bansi got some remunerative assignments from the Field Survey Organization (FSO) headed by J N Zutshi.

J N Zutshi was an ardent admirer of Bansi Parimu's work. Like Kashi Nath Bhan, Parimu was a multi-talented personality. If Bhan had sharpened his skills through rigorous training at Sir Amar Singh Technical Institute, Parimu had done it through observation and self-teaching. I know for certain that apart from painting, Bansiji could do set designing and acting. Parimu had an additional expertise in the field of photography. Kashi Nath Bhan had designed the sets of Nadim Sahib's opera *Bombur-Yemberzal*, directed by Mohan Lal Aima. Nadim Sahib, Kashi Nath Bhan and Mohan Lal Aima were great friends. Like Kashi Nath Bhan, we had a similar talented personality known as Suraj Tiku. Suraj Tiku was a trained painter from the Sir Amar Singh Technical Institute. He was also a theatre artiste and a set designer. Parimu was a regular visitor to Suraj Tiku's house. They became good friends though Suraj Tiku was older than Bansi.

Hriday Nath Jattu and Sudesh Raina told me that Parimu was often seen in Pandit Shiv Nath Raina's house at Badiyar Bala. I interviewed them in 2017 at Jammu. 'As a young boy, Bansi Parimu was often seen around the Ganpatyar area, either going to the house of S N Butt or D N Walli or Pandit Shiv Nath Raina. These places acted as his initial training centres. Later he moved to other people and also mastered his style by observation and study. He was like a free bird in the sky. No institution could put him in a cage', says Jattu. Sudesh Raina recounts:

> Young artists visited my grandfather Shiv Nath Raina (fondly called Bobuji) in his Dewankhan (drawing room) at Badiyar Bala. Bobuji was not only a great drawing master but an innovator, a model-maker, a good teacher and a promoter of art. In those days he had made a sort of art gallery where he would showcase the works of young, aspiring and budding artists. Besides his friends, a host of young artists like G R Santosh, Suraj Tiku, and Bansi Parimu came to meet and interact with

> Bobuji in his Dewankhan. During winters, Parimu came to the Dewankhan wearing the traditional pheran (a loose outer cloak) for guidance and tips on model-making. At times, he would take a model under his pheran for study at home. Those days, due to lack of training centres or institutions, learners would come to senior artists like Bobuji and these teachers would gladly pass on whatever they knew to their students. I remember a few occasions, in later years when Bansi Parimu came to meet my father Mohan Raina. They discussed matters related to art. In his youth, apart from visiting our house, Bansi Parimu was a regular visitor to S N Butt's house. My father also revealed to me that Butt had been gifted a book by Raza that had photographs of Vincent Van Gogh's sketches and paintings. That book was a great attraction for Parimu. Butt himself was always engrossed in that book.

Apart from learning from the local artists, Bansi Parimu started looking into art books, magazines, and newspapers to study and learn various techniques, forms, and styles of art. 'A young Parimu in his twenties with a keen interest in art was always seen discovering for himself new trends in painting by reading journals and books on art. The western magazines were highly sought after by the educated and the literati. Those days, periodicals reached the capital Srinagar very late. Hardly did it matter if they were outdated. A progressive and inquisitive mind like Bansi Parimu conceived new ideas by looking into these magazines', says Kapil Kaul. And these books proved very important for the inquisitive young Bansi. From these books Parimu learned the encaustic technique.

A NON-CONFORMIST CRUSADER

BANSI PARIMU WAS a restless crusader of many causes dear to him. One cause that he repeatedly spoke about was the creation of an establishment apparatus that would be sensitive to the needs of the masses in his Kashmir, who had been deprived of some basic necessities of life for long. This belief made him support any initiative that would go in favour of installing a pro-people or socialist establishment.

POLITICAL ACTIVIST

When Sheikh Mohammad Abdullah took over the reins of the government in 1947, many in his own party expected him to implement the Naya Kashmir Manifesto in the State. It was widely believed that the Naya Kashmir Manifesto was a communist document that would usher in quick social change on the ground. Josef Korbel (father of Madeleine Albright, a former US Secretary of State) described the Naya Kashmir Manifesto as a plan supporting communist ideas and predicted that Kashmir would be the first Indian State to embrace communism. The Naya Kashmir Manifesto had an all-inclusive charter for social change with an emphasis on equal rights for women and the right to work among other progressive measures. Except for land reforms, much of the Naya Kashmir Manifesto remained on paper only. It appears as if Sheikh had consigned the Naya Kashmir Manifesto document to the dustbin after hurriedly implementing the Agrarian Land Reforms in the State.

In 1953, the political regime in the State changed which created renewed expectations. Like many others, Bansi Parimu also believed that Bakshi Ghulam Mohammad would bring the desired results. He believed that the Naya Kashmir Manifesto had now been delivered into the competent hands of Bakshi Ghulam Mohammad for implementation. Bakshi Ghulam Mohammad was a different kind of leader. Apart from politics, he was a connoisseur of music and fine arts. It was during Bakshi Ghulam Mohammad's period that the Jashn-e-Kashmir festival was organised in the State in 1956. Musicians, poets, film actors and writers from across the country were invited to participate in the various events of this Jashn (celebration).

It was a major effort by Bakshi Ghulam Mohammad's government to showcase Kashmir as a tourist destination to the nation. To participate in Jashn-e-Kashmir, some prominent Hindi film stars were brought to Kashmir in a chartered plane at the government's expense. The boarding and lodging arrangements for them were also made by the government. The celebrations included many cultural programmes, a grand all-India Urdu Mushaira, boat regattas, dramas, music competitions, bicycle races, Bhaand Pather plays, Chhakri programmes, handicrafts display, a cricket match between participating film stars and many other events. Srinagar city was given a festive look. Even school children were involved in the Jashn-e-Kashmir.

After 1956, Kashmir witnessed a flow of domestic tourists. Many film units from Mumbai started coming to Kashmir for shooting Hindi films. It was Bakshi Ghulam Mohammad's initiative that attracted Bollywood to Kashmir. A very senior political leader from Kashmir had this to say: 'Bakshi Sahib must have seen Raj Kapoor's *Awaara* at least five times. In a good mood, he would sing the song, *Awaara Huun*. He was a great admirer of Raj Kapoor. During Jashn-e-Kashmir celebrations, pamphlets were distributed in the Srinagar city and huge billboards were put up at prominent places announcing the gala live performance of Raj Kapoor and Nargis. People were invited to witness the show. Inside the Hazuri Bagh park, a huge stage was created using

Deodar wood sleepers. Bakshi Sahib personally supervised the stage creation, and, in a way, he led the team. During the performance, Bakshi Sahib requested Nargis and Raj Kapoor to sing *'Ramaiya Vasta Vaiya'* and they obliged. They danced while crowds cheered them lustily. It was a new song but very popular during those days. Nargis and Raj Kapoor joined the exhibition cricket match played by the film stars. This match was also inaugurated by Bakshi Sahib. Raj Kapoor was seen with leg guards and a bat in his hand. Actor Agha and the tragedy king Dilip Kumar were also in white dresses for this exhibition match. The match was played at the JKCA ground, Chinar Bagh opposite Burn Hall School, Srinagar.'

Habib Painter Qawaal was Bakshi Ghulam Mohammad's favourite. He was also brought to participate in Jashn-e-Kashmir. He became quite popular and kept visiting Kashmir subsequently. The festivities were also held at Nishat garden (Shab-e-Nishat), Shalimar garden (Shab-e-Shalimar), Badaamwari garden, the Tourist Reception Centre, Arts Emporium ground and Srinagar's Nedous hotel.

Bakshi Ghulam Mohammad evolved his own style of functioning. He almost demolished systems and procedures in the administration by resorting to short cuts. He ordered appointments personally on representations, brushing aside educational qualifications, interviews, and eligibility criteria. Favouritism, nepotism, and corruption, that was meant to be driven away by the Naya Kashmir Manifesto[1]

1 Who wrote the Naya Kashmir Manifesto? This issue is not clear to anybody. The eminent Persian scholar and historian, Dr Kashi Nath Pandita told me that N N Raina (former HOD, Physics, University of Kashmir and a veteran communist intellectual of the State) played a pivotal role in drafting the Naya Kashmir Manifesto. Some people believe it to be the joint effort of B P L Bedi (father of actor Kabir Bedi), Freda Bedi, N N Raina, M D Taseer, Daniel Latifi and some leftists from Kashmir and Lahore. I was told that by and large, this manifesto is a copy of the constitution of the erstwhile USSR. I was also told that Gangadhar Adhikari, the well-known Marxist theoretician and writer, played a key role in getting it drafted from Stalin's new constitution. Some writers believe that it was copied from the constitution of Uzbekistan (then a State of the erstwhile USSR) and given a suitable local colour. BPL Bedi and his wife Freda did the typing and some editing to it. However, the fact remains that Maulana Masoodi, a Kashmiri politician, translated it into Urdu after it was released to the press by Bedi. BPL Bedi and his wife Freda lived in Srinagar from 1947 to 1952 and had a long association with Sheikh Abdullah's National Conference from the 1930s.

touched newer heights during Bakshi Ghulam Mohammad's rule. That created resentment in many circles, especially the communist group within the National Conference. The obvious choice for Bakshi Ghulam Mohammad's substitute was a young, honest, well-educated and suave mannered Ghulam Mohammad Sadiq. The communists within National Conference floated a new group that came to be known as the Democratic National Conference or DNC party.Bansi Parimu played a crucial role in the formation of the DNC party. He played this role to bring together like-minded leaders on a common platform for a common cause.

Bansi Parimu was very good at photography. During this period, he had purchased a good camera that he used for nature photography which was his other hobby. Now, this camera was put to some different use. This is what my interviewees had to say about Bansi Parimu's role during the formation of the DNC party:

> Paddling his bicycle, Bansi Parimu had clicked many photographs of various buildings and immovable property acquired by the brothers of Bakshi Ghulam Mohammad, allegedly through dishonest means. All these photographs were published in a booklet form that was distributed by the DNC. I possessed one booklet. I have lost it now.
>
> **—Arvind Gigoo**

> In 1957, when the DNC was launched by organising a gala event in Gole Bagh Park, Bansi was the key organiser. We experienced unusual snowfall that day. The awning fell on the ground but the organisers continued to remain at the venue in the snowfall, with Parimu persuading everybody to stay put and not to worry. We worked together for the Communist Party of India. He was also associated with the CPI newspaper, *Kashmir*. Together we sold its copies in the markets. Then I told him to be away and remain busy with his work. Those were the formative years of the DNC in Kashmir. Many meetings of the DNC took place

in his Habba Kadal room cum studio. That ordinary room was his studio, meeting place and bedroom. That time he had not shifted to his new Barzulla house. He was a bachelor. M L Misri, K D Sethi, Syed Mir Qasim, Ram Pyara Saraf and many other leaders have visited that room. Anybody who was somebody in the State's political hierarchy has visited that room including two former chief ministers. He was always selfless. He thought of amelioration of the sufferings of a common Kashmiri. And communism was great hope. He had a very good camera that was used to capture images of events and episodes. That camera did some wonders for the DNC.

—Capt S K Tikoo

In 1957, Bansi Parimu was closely associated with the formation of the DNC party, a splinter group of the J&K National Conference, created by the leftists within the party and headed by G M Sadiq. The DNC party stood for the extension of the central laws to Kashmir. This group was to dislodge Bakshi Ghulam Mohammad later. Parimu would prepare posters and pamphlets for the DNC party and then distribute them together with his friends right from Lal Chowk to Safakadal. The Jammu group of the DNC party was led by Ram Payara Saraf. I have seen Saraf also inside his small room at Habba Kadal that was his studio cum activity space. He would move with M L Misri, N N Raina, D P Dhar, G M Sadiq and many other known leftist leaders from Kashmir. Later, I saw him as a close associate of Shamim Ahmed Shamim, MP.

—Hriday Nath Jattu

Initially, Bansi Parimu had taken a room on rent. The room was located on the upper story of the shop of Ali Mohd and Sons (Booksellers), Habba Kadal. From that place, he then shifted to his own room that he set up as a studio cum living room.

> His friends and guests always came to that room. That room was visited by D P Dhar, M L Misri, Syed Mir Qasim, Abdul Aziz Haroon, Pran Nath Jalali, G R Renzu, Dina Nath Nadim and many people who were either politicians or communists or artists. It was an ordinary house at Habba Kadal in Srinagar city. The DNC was born in Bansi Parimu's room cum studio. Bansi and his friends would make posters and publicity material for the DNC party in that room. Bansi would distribute the DNC party posters on his bicycle. The DNC party was against Bakshi Ghulam Mohammad and had the patronage of G M Sadiq.
>
> **—M K Tikoo**

Consequent to implementation of the Kamaraj Plan, Bakshi Ghulam Mohammad had to resign and G M Sadiq took over the reins of the State. As soon as this happened, Bansi Parimu, a close confidant of Sadiq, started distancing himself from the power circle. He had understood the limitations of the DNC that came to power in Kashmir. Sadiq, in spite of being honest and secular in his dealings and outlook, allowed himself to be surrounded by some sycophants. His sister Zainab Begum started using her power and created her clout to influence the administration. Sadiq also inducted a rich relative from the Burza family into the seat of power. Tirath Ram Amla, another wealthy businessman, was inducted into the assembly. These actions were considered pro-capitalist by many political observers and workers in the field. During this period, Bansi Parimu came closer to Shamim Ahmed Shamim, a new hope emerging on Kashmir's political horizon. Shamim was young, outspoken, sharp, witty and well-read. Shamim was a gifted writer, fearless editor and lover of urdu poetry and literature. He was an independent MLA, known for his oratory and walkouts from the J&K assembly proceedings. Later, he represented Srinagar constituency in the Lok Sabha. This was also the period when Parimu came closer to Syed Mir Qasim, Mir Mustafa and Peer Hassam-ud-Din, a de facto anti-Sadiq camp in the government.

Arvind Gigoo narrates an anecdote relating to Sadiq during this period:

> G M Sadiq was a seasoned politician and a great administrator. He had the knack of owning and disowning people without hitting anybody directly. Though Bansi Parimu was very close to Sadiq at one point in time, later, for some reason, Sadiq tried to distance himself from Parimu. In a function at Srinagar's then upmarket Tourist Reception Centre, Sadiq was personally received by Parimu in his capacity as principal host of the function. In that function, Sadiq met him in a way so as to give an impression that he did not know Bansi Parimu at all. '*Van sa Chaman Lal*' or 'How are you Chaman Lal?', said Sadiq. Astonished at this, Parimu had to retort, 'Sadiq Sahib, I am Bansi Parimu. How come you forget my name?' Without responding, Sadiq moved ahead and sat on the dais.

Bansi Parimu was a rebel. He did not seek any favour from any friend in the government. D P Dhar, who later moved to Indira Gandhi's cabinet, remained an ardent admirer of Bansi Parimu's art and his role in establishing the DNC party. Parimu distanced himself from Dhar too. Parimu's friends recall:

> He was a non-conformist from childhood. In later years of his life, it became a part of his personality. Never ever has he sought a favour for himself. Sometimes his rebellious temperament did not go down well with some petty bureaucrats. I remember, his wife Jaya Parimu was transferred to Baramulla as some senior bureaucrat wanted to settle scores with Bansi. But he never approached any person to get her transferred back.
>
> **—Capt S K Tikoo**

> Though he was very close to D P Dhar yet on some principles, once he went against him as well. I vividly remember how in 1967, Bansi Parimu did a mural-type of creation with empty glass bottles

> and hung it on the railings of the Habba Kadal bridge. It carried a satirical note against Dhar who happened to be a minister at that time. There was no malice in Parimu's action. His respect, affection and regard for Dhar remained unabated. In fact, Bansi Parimu had expressed his resentment against the then government. And D P Dhar was truly a liberal, gracious and an open-minded person who never got offended. When Parimu met Dhar later, everything was normal as usual. He had understood Bansi Parimu's compulsions. Dhar even turned more affectionate towards him.
>
> **—Makhan Lal Saraf**

CIVIL SOCIETY ACTIVIST AND ENVIRONMENTALIST

In spite of his serious engagement with art, politics remained a passion for Bansi Parimu. After the Indira-Sheikh accord of 1975, Sheikh Abdullah held the reins of Kashmir once more. Sheikh already knew Parimu for his work as a National Conference activist before 1953. He was always treated as a VIP at the 'Chief Minister's Private Office'. Later, during Farooq Abdullah's rule, Bansi Parimu took up many other causes dear to him.

He was deeply connected with INTACH's Kashmir Chapter, the Urban Arts Council, the Parihaaspora Task Force, State's Environment and Ecology Protection Council, Academy of Art, Culture, and Languages, the Institute of Music and Fine Arts (visiting faculty); Wild Life Protection, Dal Development, Protection of Cultural and Architectural Heritage of the State and some other public causes. He also started associating with some national newspapers to express his political opinions. His analytical interviews, based on ground realities, had many admirers. These were treated as realistic feedbacks for arriving at many crucial decisions on Kashmir. He continued this activity even when he began to live in Delhi after 1990.

Jaya Parimu has this anecdote to narrate:

> I had once gone to my friend and colleague Suraiya's (Farooq Abdullah's younger sister) house where we were having tea with

two more colleagues in the garden adjacent to Farooq's house when Farooq Abdullah suddenly dropped in. He had flown back from Delhi and was heavily garlanded. As he entered, he straightway told me, *'Parimu Saeban Bachaav Kasheer'* or 'Parimu Sahib has saved Kashmir'. I will elaborate on the background of Farooq Abdullah's statement. Bansi Parimu held an exhibition of his paintings (perhaps in 1986) at Lalit Kala Akademi. During that exhibition, he was interviewed by some journalists. In these interviews, he gave his opinion on the art and politics of Kashmir. One interview, that got published in a national daily, was read by Sonia Gandhi. This interview created some interest in Sonia Gandhi, and she visited Lalit Kala Akademi to see Parimu's art exhibition. She then invited Parimu to her office and had some conversation with him on art and Kashmir politics. Parimu was always sincere and passionate about Kashmir. His inputs left an impact that worked in favour of the reinstallation of the government headed by Farooq Abdullah. Bansi Parimu had told Farooq Abdullah about his meeting with Sonia Gandhi. He never took any credit for anything that he did selflessly.

Visual art has the power to impact the environment, as well as raise awareness of the environmental problems and help the decision-makers in the environmental dominion. History has many examples of artists contributing positively towards environmental concerns. Through their dedicated and selfless efforts, many artists have become major links between society and the environment. In Kashmir, Bansi Parimu played a key role in this arena.

His political activities were never meant to achieve proximity to Power. Bansi Parimu was always interested in the welfare of the common man. He was a free crusader. In 1975, Sheikh, Abdullah wanted to convert the Arts Emporium building and the entire premises into Tehzeeb Mahal, a huge cultural centre. Even architects were retained to design it. Bansi Parimu started a

> crusade against the idea fearing all the lofty Chinar trees would be cut and the heritage garden complex in the heart of the city would be converted into a concrete structure. The proposal did not move ahead.
>
> **—Pran Kishore Kaul**

While art and painting remained close to his heart, Kashmir remained embedded in his soul. Till his death, he remained steadfast in his concern for his birthplace. Any endeavour that meant the development of his birthplace or welfare of its inhabitants was something that he volunteered to associate with. His association did not simply mean meetings and passing resolutions. It meant swift action that generally bypassed routine bureaucratic hurdles and impediments. His deep, sincere and selfless involvement with a cause that was close to his heart got him connected to many societies, groups and committees. As a leader of the 'Save Chinar' movement, he made strenuous efforts to save the Chinar trees that were being cut for widening roads and other construction activities.

Deeply anguished at the destruction of the flora and fauna in his homeland, he expressed his anguish in an interview that appeared in a leading English newspaper published from New Delhi. He pointed out:

> Historical manuals, including Rajatarangini, give a detailed account of the vast orchards with juicy fruits and sweet grapes. Today, almost all the indigenous varieties of fruits have vanished. According to records, the Mughals left behind 500 gardens. The existing seven have nothing Mughal in them. Srinagar is perhaps the world's only city where without any industrialisation, pollution is an enormous problem.

He was always annoyed over the government's apathy, callousness, and neglect towards the environment. His daughter Jheelaf Parimu Razdan recalls, 'He was admitted to AIIMS, and within 24 hours he was gone. On his way to the hospital in the taxi, even when he was in pain, he kept looking out of the window pointing towards some vacant land and suggesting that something could be built there to save the area from becoming a concrete jungle. He was a true environmentalist'.

A newspaper published from Srinagar, *The Greater Kashmir*, wrote on 31 May 2012:

> Observers said that in 1984, the then government led by Ghulam Mohammad Shah had conceived the idea to construct a bridge across Jhelum at Polo View. But as the construction would spoil The Bund – the heritage walkway – on the river banks, the move was resisted tooth-and-nail by the then civil society, particularly art lovers. Bansi Parimu had threatened to go for self-immolation, should the government go ahead with the plan. Parimu is believed to have started a campaign that the concrete bridge would destroy the charm of the only green walkway left in the city.

Makhan Lal Saraf told me:

> Bansi was a lover of nature, environment, flora, and fauna of Kashmir. One day, while walking along the Bund, he discussed a plan with me as to how the city of Srinagar could be saved from the fury of floods. He gave many ideas while we walked. These ideas were brilliant. While I was listening to him, I kept thinking about my role in a play that I had to perform at the Tagore Hall the next day. Now I realise how serious his concerns were. While he thought about future events, we were busy thinking about tomorrow at the most.

Bashir Budgami, a retired senior official of Doordarshan, wrote on a Facebook post:

> During the days of *'Grees Gand'*, the Kisan movement in Kashmir, Bansi Parimu used to visit Budgam frequently. He was

supporting the agitating farmers. He was as good as a family member and always loved me. I did a couple of programmes about him and his works later, when I became a producer at the Srinagar Kendra of Doordarshan.

MULTIFACETED ARTIST

After G M Sadiq, Syed Mir Qasim took over the reins of the State. By this time Parimu had already got deeply involved and busy in his artistic pursuits. He had also acquired practical knowledge of interior decoration, landscaping, and architecture. Some exhibitions in Mumbai, Kolkata, Amritsar, Hyderabad, and New Delhi won him many admirers from among some leading artists of the country who saw his work. By now corruption was deeply entrenched in the State's administration. He started distancing himself from active politics and focusing on his work. And by the dint of his hard work and artistic dexterity, Parimu attracted the attention of well-known artist N S Bendre. He invariably met Bendre whenever he went to Mumbai. Tyeb Mehta was another artist who saw excellent potential and merit in Parimu's work. He suggested to Parimu that he should shift to some bigger city so that his work could be widely seen. 'Yes, Tyeb Mehta appreciated his work', recalls Jaya Parimu.

Jaya adds, 'Sometime around 1971, Tyeb Mehta along with his family visited Kashmir to participate in an art camp at Ganderbal. Parimu also joined that camp. I vividly remember many pleasant moments spent with Tyeb Mehta and his wife. We grew friendly with that family. I remember those tonga rides with Parimu, and Tyeb Mehta clicking our photos. I have lost all those great photographs in the turmoil that made us leave Kashmir. Tyeb Mehta's wife spent some good time with us. Parimu kept in touch with Tyeb.

'I vividly remember that lunch at K K Hebber's Kalanagar house was a must whenever we were in Mumbai. Hebber also appreciated what Parimu had been doing. Hebber had studied art at Paris and during his formative years, he was influenced by Paul Gauguin and

Amrita Shergill. Then I remember Bal Chhabra. He would not allow Parimu to leave Mumbai unless he had lunch with him. So was it with Krishen Khanna and Husain, who lived at Colaba. They were equally cordial and affectionate to Parimu. Souza, Raza, Satish Gujral, Ram Kumar, B C Sanyal, Bimal Dasgupta, Sachinda Nagdev and Shanti Dave were also Parimu's friends. Sanyal was a very senior and highly respected person. After Parimu's death, Sanyal personally visited us in Delhi to offer his condolences. G R Santosh was like a brother to Parimu. While In Delhi, lunch or dinner at Santosh's house was a must in our schedule.

'Bansi Parimu had very cordial relations with Husain. Every time Husain came to Kashmir, Parimu was his companion. Even his son, artist Shamshad, had cordial and family ties with the Parimus. Like Tyeb Mehta, Husain would always advise Parimu to shift to some metropolitan city to be visible. In Srinagar, Parimu was M F Husain's companion. We had cordial relations with the entire Husain family. Husain dominated the national art scene for so many years, yet he was an extremely simple man. He ate very little and loved green leafy Kohlrabi (Monji in Kashmiri) cooked in Kashmiri style. He always carried this vegetable to Mumbai from Kashmir. We saw him last in 1989 when he visited our house at Barzulla. Husain loved to play with children. He spoke to the children in their language. He would always say that childhood is the only malice-free period in a man's life. He painted a dancing Ganesha and horses for our children. They remain our family's prized possessions. Even Shamshad's father-in-law had family ties with us. We spent a very good time together. The Baroda-trained sculptor Vidya Ratan Khajuria was a close friend of Parimu. He had a sumptuous Kashmiri dinner at our house in 1989. That day he had a long discussion with Parimu on the art scenario in our State. I feel sad to relate all these past stories. It is really painful for exiles like me', says Jaya Parimu.

Khajuria was an admirer of Parimu's work. When Khajuria died (1934-1990), Parimu wrote an emotional tribute to the sculptor that was published by the *Kashmir Times* in 1990. And in 1991, Parimu followed him to his heavenly abode. Both died young.

Parimu enjoyed his friendship with Sachida Nagdev (1939-2017), the well-known artist of the abstract genre from Ujjain. Nagdev was an admirer of Parimu's work. At that time, Nagdev was considered synonymous with Indian abstract art. Like Parimu, Nagdev's abstracts are open to multiple interpretations and his colours, especially greens, reds and blues weave magic with their rhythmic patterns and sensitive textural quality.

Another artist with whom Bansi Parimu had perfect compatibility and friendship was Bimal Dasgupta[2] (1917-1995). Dasgupta is hailed as one of Bengal's leading abstract painters. When Dasgupta saw some abstract exhibitions by Parimu, he was impressed. Some of Dasgupta's abstracts look similar to Parimu's work. Possibly, both spoke to their inner being in the same language. Bimal Dasgupta did murals, watercolours, installations and oil paintings. He was a fellow of Lalit Kala Akademi and taught at the Delhi College of Art.

2 One oil on canvas titled 'Reminiscence (painting) - 1965' done by Bimal Dasgupta is on display at Lalit Kala Akademi, New Delhi. This painting looks like an abstraction done by Bansi Parimu. Again, another painting of Bimal Dasgupta titled 'Blue landscape 1964' closely resembles Parimu's abstract style. Was Parimu influenced by Bimal Dasgupta's style? This needs a detailed study and exploration.

THE HINDU
India's National Newspaper
Delhi Edition
Printed at Madras, Coimbatore, Bangalore, Hyderabad, Madurai, Gurgaon and Visakhapatnam

CUS

Bansi Parimu: Artist and activist

A sound theory, Karl Popper emphasized, 'is characterized by the fact that it makes a number of predictions that could in principle be disproved or falsified by observation'. But stages of development of the art of Bansi Parimu run contra to Wilhelm Worringer's historically sound theory that in periods when man is at home in his world, naturalistic art flourishes, and that in periods when man is alarmed by his world, non-figurative or abstract art appears.

Pansi Parimu, the noted Kashmiri artist who died in New Delhi on July 29 last year had been turning out scintillating abstract paintings during the seventies and early eighties, happy in his picturesque residence 'Takhleeque' (creation) in Srinagar. Later, when Kashmir became a 'problem', when terror struck the

ART with Santo Datta

Valley, we see in his paintings the anguished onrush of a gory reality, the disquieting images of the collapse of a fine culture, of a people uprooted in waves of violence. Bansi 'proved' the soundness of Worringer's theory by falsifying it. In his canvases the retreat from the reality was replaced by images of life bleeding in the sun.

On the evening of July 29, eminent artists, critics, art lovers, friends and relations gathered at the All India Fine Arts and Crafts Society, Rafi Marg, to observe the first anniversary of the death of the artist. Most of the speakers dwelt at length on his courage and his deep love of the valley and its people. He never wanted to leave the Valley he loved so much, never thought of migrating to the Capital, and he stuck to his decision till he was compelled

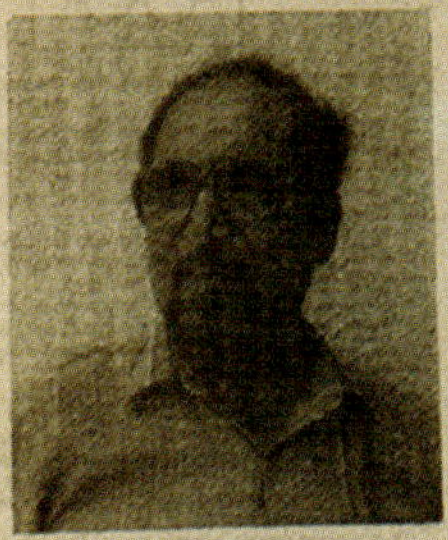

by the political situation to leave behind everything he loved and cherished — his studio 'Tassawur' (imagination), his home 'Takhleeque', his garden of flowers, and his people. He succumbed to a minor wound he had neglected, which turned gangrenous. The end was sudden.

Born in 1933 in Srinagar, Bansi Parimu was a self-taught painter and sculptor. He was a prolific writer, campaigning for the solution of the prpblems of the people, writing tirelessly on the increasingly alarming environmental pollution in Kashmir.

By the mid-fifties, Bansi appeared on the contemporary Indian art scene as a professional artist. Recognition came to him in the sixties and seventies. He won first prize in J & K Academy Exhibitions in 1960, '68, '69, '70 and '71. The Madhya Pradesh Kala Parishad, the Indian Academy of Art, Amritsar, the AIFACS, New Delhi, and the Academy of Fine Arts, Calcutta, honoured him for his artistic contributions.

One of his memorable contributions is the initiation of an on-going programme of holding annual artists camp in Srinagar, in which artists invited from all parts of the country participated. His objective was to start interaction between the artists of Kashmir and those from the other States. Lately this has been discontinued.

A campaigner against environmental pollution, Bansi Parimu once wrote in an English daily in the Capital: 'Historic manuals, including the 'Rajatarangini', give a detailed account of the vast orchards with juicy fruits and sweets grapes. Today almost all the indigenous varieties of fruit have vanished. According to records, the Mughals left behind over 500 gardens. The existing seven now have nothing Mughal in them.... Srinagar is perhaps the world's only city where without any industrialisation, pollution is an enormous problem'. A committed activist, he literally writhed in anguish and anger — anger against communalism, against Governmental callousness.

Last year, in an interview, Bansi was asked why he had refused to accept the migrant's allowance. He replied: 'It is so humiliating. Anyone with self-respect will not seek it'. And then, he said: 'I am planning to work on a large painting and a few posters on Kashmir. One theme can be, donkeys grazing on a field of saffron'.

Lively paintings by Bansi Parimu

Recent paintings of Bansi Parimu, the noted painter from Kashmir, are now presented by Dhoomi Mal Gallery at Connaught Place. Bansi Parimu's paintings belong to that movement of abstract art in India which liberated the form and colour from the age-old associations with recognisable subject-matter, literary content and traditional linkages between the natural shapes and local colours.

As the late Jaya Appaswamy analysed it correctly, the abstract art, with its new set of pictorial values, came to India around the fifties not inspired by the contemporary movement of abstract expressionism, but was inspired by the works of Kandinsky and Paul Klee. And it struck its first roots in the fifties when pioneers of modern Indian art were breaking down forms to colour

Art

planes and spatial arrangements. The works of Bansi Parimu belong to this long line of experiments with new aesthetic experience.

The painter, despite a long spell of disabling arthritis, has been painting with an uncanny devotion found usually among religious thinkers. Compared to his earlier paintings, the recent ones are less heavy with coloured wax. In fact, the coloured wax is used for sinuous linear movements, giving the total compositions an unobstrusive but lively linear accents, the kind we admired in the lacquered Ukiyo-e woodblock prints of the late 18th and 19th centuries Japan.

Bansi Parimu's w rks, if the viewer insists on having a explanation or meaning, are more suggestive of the ceaseless change in he micro-life in nature, than the architectonic abstractions of Piet Mondrian lineage. They are more poetic in the line of Kandinsky in their areas of tensions of colours, than the linear intellectual whimsies' of Paul Klee.

In fact, the artist has successfully hidden the structure of tensions between colour-fields and linear movements, and has given his works a kind of spontaneity, a feeling of fortuitous relationships between different degrees of tensions on the surface. The patient viewer will notice particularly his use of tonality which never dominates the colour areas, instead the tones always appear subservient to lines which, in their turn, bring in the abstract forms. This has given his paintings the charm of viscosity prints, luminous but not flashy.

One of his finest paintings on view is No. 16: the linear skein brings out the highly contrasting areas in black and red, making a straightforward pictorial statement we sometimes find in woodblock prints. Some canvases suggest processes of transformation in explosive arrangement of linear flows, and soft curves of oval, and rounded-off rectangles are sometimes compressed, as if under great pressure. This movement, this complex patterns of tensions are the real charm of Bansi Parimu's abstract paintings. Another feature has been subtly used to add to the richness and complexity of surface tensions, that is, the dry brush texture showing the thread-pattern of the canvas. In his earlier paintings, the use of wax softened and polished the colour areas. This time it is more direct, more spontaneous.

Among other canvases, Nos. 5 and 14 show what this indefatigable abstract painter can do w h liberated forms, lines and colours.

On view till 31 December.

— SANTO DATTA

THE TIMES OF INDIA, NEW DELHI WEDNESDAY, FEBRUARY 26 1992

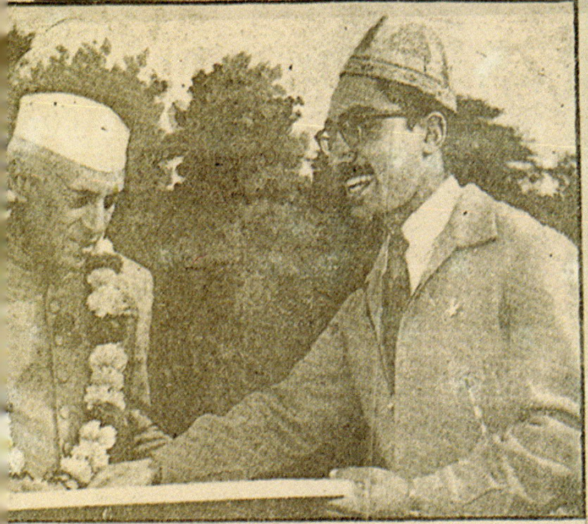

...ru admiring a painting by Bansi Parimu

Parimu's lament for Kashmir

REVIEW
ART

Bansi Parimu
Dhoomi Mal Gallery

THIS commemorative exhibition is at once elevating and depressing for those who saw a happy valley become the apple of discord. Parimu, a good painter, was also an outspoken, independent-minded being. The loss to the community of his personal presence, as of his creative imagination, cannot therefore be denied. Those who gathered at the opening of this show expressed their distress as well as appreciation of the man unambiguously.

Though this exhibition is timely, the painter's works scattered all over J&K and here need a better, a more thoroughly selected exhibition. It presents a body of work which he did after those red patches on white snow (Smeared Snows') but also compositions which celebrate eternal life. The best of these latter works honour, in their own terms -- the terms of contemporary space art -- the spirit of delight which is reflected at its tantalizing best in the valley and its waters. A nature in love -- soft and gentle -- which once brought about a feeling of trust in its humans. The painter would most assuredly have meditated on those famed lakes that in summer are like vast sheets of broken glass, and on the poplars that look like fingers pointing towards the sun high above the brightly curving hills.

Parimu's work then is a mathematical token of the soft fall of the shikara oars -- its slow progress emphasising the quality of sacredness one associates with things of the risen spirit. Nothing, in the best of Parimu's homage to the goddess with the musical instrument, is erratic, frantic, rough, rude or boisterous. But was not that another day?

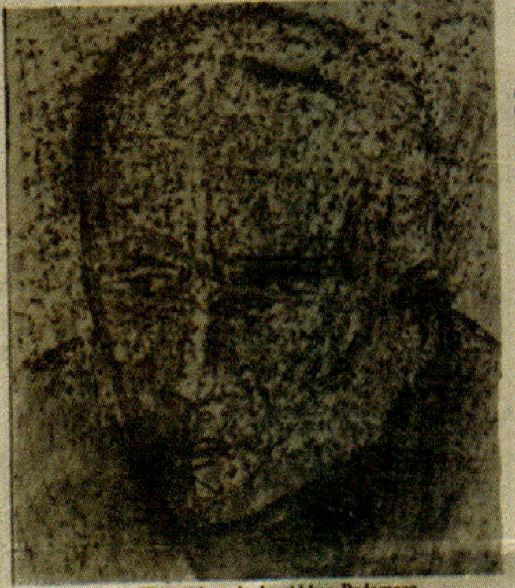

A Charcoal study by Akbar Padamsee

AUSTERE MOOD

Akbar Padamsee
Art Heritage

These charcoal works, though physically light, are in fact weighty with the weight of a controlled feeling. The painter who oscillates between abstract landscape and the theme of the martyrdom of the son god, or the solemnity connected with that moment, is really best in figuration -- that is if one were obliged to make a choice. His sculpted heads, seen earlier, and now these austere, most frugal charcoals, show that he is the same man he was many years ago. But these fresh figurations are more mature, probably due to a perfected technique and greater reticence. Such austerity is just right for the times we live in. His method, as if a kind of eruption on the surface of the canvas, does not betoken corruption but the determination to bear pain and humiliation with the legendary Christian forebearance. Of course, physiognomically, the expressions here are a trifle outlandish, as earlier. But that is a minor point.

CONTROLLED FEELING

Vivan Sundaram
Shridharani Gallery

One thing is the art of thought: another thought as art. Still another art is a dumb thing, in that it cannot be easily transcribed into words, being merely an aroma which overcomes you. In this presentation the artist has many supporters, some of who are proficient in the art of presentation itself, of designing and of building. All these require a great deal of thought and somewhat less of that sleepwalker's tread whereby the last named order of art comes about.

Here ideas are tried out with an eye on the public -- in the main. The art of architecture and designing are the mega voice, and these come in handy for this genre of art, of either expressing ideas or using materials which stem from both, the neolithic economy as the very brainy, computer age one. These combinations are perhaps devised to stimulate the smug moderns. In this strategy there is much seeming freedom of choice, and much that will appear sensational to the dull. By taking thought you can invent that which assists your droopy anima to get out of the grooves of set art. But the exercise is functional, in essentials an adjunct or first course to art proper. The thing is cunningly done. Particularly good are the sandstone pillars and the mirror boxes. The former approaches the quality permanent art in certain ways.

SYMBOLIC TRADITION

Graphics from Egypt
Azad Bhavan

Some excellent work is to be seen in this show from the land of the Sphinx. The Delhi Egyptian embassy building has a calligraphic form; so too have some of the works in this show, which are

EVENING NEWS
THE HINDUSTAN TIMES
Vol. XLIX No. 182 New Delhi Friday, July 31 1992 12 Pages Rs 1.50

Bansi Parimu's legacy

...I PARIMU and the ...us nature of Kashmir are ...ably linked to one another, ...ally impossible to think of ...out the other. In fact Ban...so committed an environ...st that such an equation ...ure was bound to develop ...e years.

...er colourist and a sensitive ...aving his fingers on the ...life in the Valley, Bansi, as ...known to his close friends, ...ive, and justifiably so, on ...onts at the same time—..., the environment and the ...of Kashmir. He painted ...as the most alluring thing in ...ashmir Valley—its nature ... landscape; he discussed ...as the most engaging issue ...Valley—Kashmiri life, peo...politics; and he wrote ab...at was ailing Kashmir and ...ts people were being ...d; and, lastly, he fought ...hout his life to preserve the ... environment of the gem ... the Valley.

...ay be debatable as to how ...ucceeded in his efforts con...

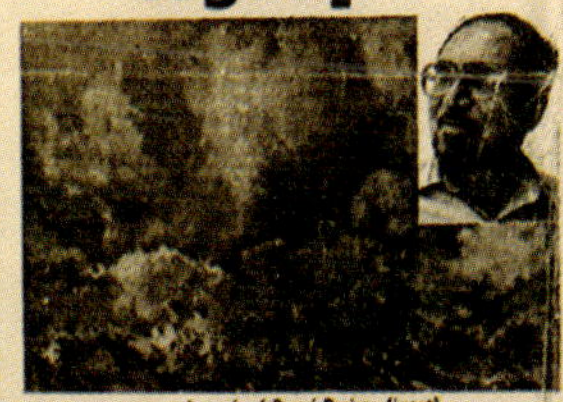

A work of Bansi Parimu (inset)

celebrity. In fact Bansi Parimu's contribution to the aforesaid three aspects of Kashmiri life is so substantial that it would take years for caringly done canvases—all those fleeting moments of colour and the feelings induced by them. However, it was not a sudden

Done in the abstract vein, Bansi's landscapes unfold before the viewer — the irresistible poetry of colours and an engaging orchestration of lines. Rich in emotional content, they transport the viewer into a different world — the world of the Sufi saints or that of the Indian Vaishnavites, wherein love and devotion alone, rule.

Organically structured to perfection, these soule-filling chromatic psalms are an unique experience for the viewer to confront and absorb. These creations of Bansi also release the inner being and rearrange his core with qualitatively different stuff. For these are the outcome of his ordeal before his easel and canvas.

During the last days of his life, Bansi was greatly troubled by the developing crisis in the gem-like precious valley of Kashmir — the growing terrorism, separatism and bloodshed (the crisis that made him and his family, alongwith the thousands of his Kashmiri brethren, refugees in his own country.)

THURSDAY 20 DECEMBER 20...

Artistic visions from the Valley

Artist BANSI PARIMU's artworks have always brought out the best of the Kashmir landscapes. His daughter CHANDRIKA P has organised a special tribute to his work with an exhibition at the Artists' Centre, Ador House, Kala Ghoda. Parimu, a self-taught artist, founded the Kashmir Fine Art Society and the Young Artistes Club. Parimu's abstracts reflect the turmoil within

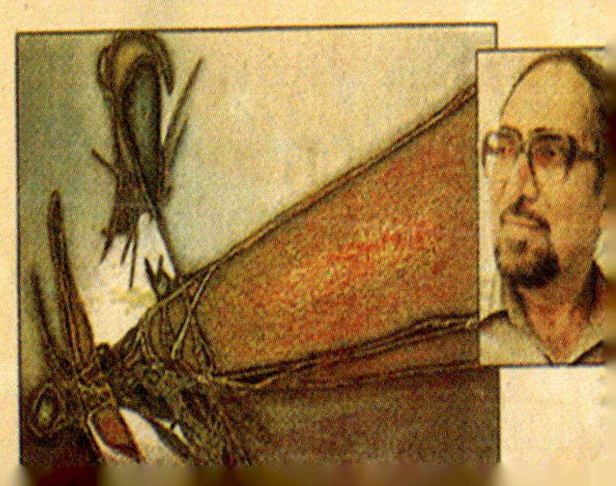

COFFEE HOUSE DAYS

RAFIQ RAAZ, THE well-known Kashmiri poet, laments upon many things that were cleared from the landscape and social life of Kashmir by armed militancy of 1990s. He writes:

Daarie bur taalav ta pash dewaar leikh
Yuss shahar gum gav tamiek aasaar leikh
Daamanas pyaath soantiki sabzaar leikh
Doann achhan manz aab ki phanwaar leikh

Write these windows, doors, ceiling, roof and the walls;
should you write the story of the city that vanished,
then write these as the monuments.
Should you write about our clothing,
write greenery of the spring season;
But when you write about these two eyes,
write tears hurrying down like fountains.

The India Coffee House on the Residency Road in Srinagar was always crowded with writers, poets, painters, dramatists, artists, musicians, politicians, journalists, college teachers, strugglers and men from other social groups. Many people sat there chatting, smoked and sipped inexpensive but excellentiy brewed coffee, served smilingly by ever-busy waiters. One could also order a Dosa or Vada or Idli and even buy coffee seeds. M L Channa, a local Kashmiri, was the manager.

The playwright Ali Mohammad Lone once admitted that he conceived the plots of his popular dramas in this coffee house. The regular visitors to the India Coffee House, Srinagar included the Sahitya Akademi awardee short story writer Akhtar Mohi-ud-Din, poet Amin Kamil, Sattar Ahmed Shahid (Urdu professor), Surrender Tikoo (botany professor), Trilok Dass (actor), Omkar Aima (actor), artist G R Santosh (whenever in Srinagar), Shafi Shaida (poet and a political leader), Arvind Gigoo (English professor), Pran Nath Jalali (journalist), Abdul Majeed Baba (businessman), Zaffar Meraj (journalist), Wahid Raina (industrialist and political activist), Shamim Ahmed Shamim (journalist and later MP), Mohammad Syeed Malik (journalist), Brij Bhardwaj (journalist), Inder Dev Sanyal (dancer), artist M F Husain (whenever in Srinagar) and many more.

Bansi Parimu was a regular visitor to the India Coffee House. He would come around 11 am. Quite often, he came straight to the India Coffee House after dropping off his wife at the gate of the Women's College on Maulana Azad Road, where she taught music.

If one wanted to locate Parimu in the city, India Coffee House was the place. Parimu had proficiency in many fields like cinema, art, Urdu poetry, music. classical dance, journalism, and architecture. The subjects that drew a crowd to his table in the coffee house were environment and civil rights in Kashmir. Bansi Parimu's company was sought by many at the India Coffee House. His friends in the India Coffee House always looked for him at the table. If he was there, they stepped in, and if he was not there, they asked the manager, 'Has Parimu Sahib come today?'

'Please have your seat. He will be here soon.' Even Husain came to the India Coffee House to find him. During one summer, I saw barefooted Husain enter the Coffee House at 1 pm. He straightaway went to the manager and asked, 'Is Bansi here?' That day Parimu had gone to some shop with Abdul Majid Baba, a businessman, and later he met Husain near Preco Studio, a photographer's shop below the Coffee House. While Baba went upstairs, Husain and Bansi went somewhere else. I saw them walking near the Linz Cafe. Finally, they entered the Emporium Garden.

Inside the India Coffee House, I have seen Bansi Parimu explaining something to his friends with a sheet of paper in his hand. He would draw something on the sheet of the paper and show it to all. They responded in astonished acknowledgement. This drawing could be the architecture of a building, a human figure, a flower bed, a plan to remove the city's traffic congestion, an outline of some settlement or anything. That was his style of explaining.

> He was a regular visitor to India Coffee House in Srinagar. It was not for gossip but for another passion. He had a serious concern for the environment and civil rights. His table had the largest gathering, and he was the centre of attraction. He was into so many societies and bodies for that reason. I mean, bodies like Save Chinar, Save Hangul, Parihaaspora Task Force, Urban Arts Council, INTACH and others.
>
> **—Shantiveer Kaul**

> He had a big circle of friends both within and outside the State. They were writers, artists, politicians, and intellectuals. Riyaz Punjabi and Shamim Ahmed Shamim were very close to him. He valued this friendship and loved both of them. In the India Coffee House, I saw him in the company of Shamim Ahmed Shamim, Riyaz Punjabi, Abdul Majid Baba, Ali Mohammad Lone and others. He was the soul of any group discussion. Sometimes he would be in the Coffee House for more than six hours.
>
> **—Makhan Lal Saraf**

> The Coffee House was a place where we met every day. Bansi Parimu had many concerns, many issues close to his heart and all of them were for the welfare of the common man in Kashmir. Husain always looked for Parimu whenever he entered the India Coffee House in Srinagar. 'How are you, captain? Where is

Bansi?' would be his question.

Husain disliked sitting in the hall. He disliked sitting in any gossip gathering inside the Coffee House. Husain disliked the noise and the cigarette smoke inside the Coffee House. He would pull me out from a gathering and say, 'come, Captain, let us go to the balcony. Let us wait for Bansi over there.' Shamim Ahmed Shamim, Ali Mohammad Lone, Sham Lal Zewan, Peer Ghias-ud-Din, G R Santosh and Abdul Majeed Baba sat with Bansi Parimu almost regularly. In the Coffee House, Parimu had developed a close rapport with Brij Bhardwaj, the *Hindustan Times* correspondent.

—Capt S K Tikoo

I am naive about art, but I knew the artist Bansi Parimu closely. He was a warm, affectionate and knowledgeable person. He had vast social interactions. He was loved by one and all. I sat with him daily in the vibrant hall of the India Coffee House in Srinagar. I learned much from him. We talked about various social, political and literary issues. He had his own unique style. We lived like a family. I remember those golden and sweet interactions. I met him daily. He was anti-fascist, progressive and secular to the core. I also remember Shamim Ahmad Shamim, Ali Mohammad Lone, Pran Nath Jalali, Wahid Raina, Amin Kamil, G R Santosh and many others who are no more. God bless their souls.

—Abdul Wahid

senior physician SKIMS, Soura, Srinagar

In Srinagar, India Coffee House was closed in January 1990. It never opened thereafter. After moving to Delhi, Bansi Parimu started visiting the Coffee House at Cannaught Place, New Delhi where he endeared himself to a galaxy of writers, artists, and civil society members.

ARCHITECT, JOURNALIST AND PHOTOGRAPHER

Bansi Parimu was an excellent photographer and a skilled journalist. He was a member of the team of journalists that was sent to various States by the J&K government in 1965. This team included some known journalists of the State like Sufi Ghulam Mohammad (Editor, *The Srinagar Times*), Ved Bhasin (Editor, *The Kashmir Times*) and Shamim Ahmed Shamim (Editor, *The Aaina*, Urdu and the then Lok Sabha MP from Srinagar).

After 1990, when he moved to Delhi, he gave many interviews that were published in the newspapers. He also wrote columns for some newspapers. He developed close association with Delhi based journalists like M L Kotru, K L Kaul, Ayesha Kagal, Sabina Sehgal, Anil Maheshwari and Keshav Malik. In Srinagar, his friends from the journalist fraternity were J N Sathu, Shamim Ahmed Shamim, Sufi Ghulam Mohammad, V K Dethe and Brij Bhardwaj.

In UAE, he handled some challenging assignments of architecture and town planning. In 1991, he was also invited by the royal family of Jodhpur to act as a consultant for the restoration of Umaid Bhawan Palace. He visited Jodhpur with several ideas that could not see the light of the day due to his untimely death.

> Bansi Parimu was an ace photographer. He is the first photographer to document the pain and suffering of Kashmiris. He was the first person to click photographs of the camps of displaced Kashmiri Pandits in Jammu. Most of the photographs of 1990 or 1991 that are being circulated in the social media were clicked by him.
>
> **—Agni Shekhar**

> Bansiji's camera work was equally artistic. So was his writing. If he were not an artist, he could have been an amazing photographer or a skilled journalist.
>
> **—Shantiveer Kaul**

His write-ups or interviews published in some national newspapers were analytical and based on ground realities. Many national leaders read them. The peace and welfare of the masses was the bottom line of his writings and political commentaries. He had no personal interest.

—Capt S K Tikoo

I am certain that if he were not an artist, he would have been a photographer and an accomplished one. He had an imported camera when he was unmarried. I am lucky to have been photographed by him with that camera. He could have been a successful journalist as well. He photographed the immovable properties owned by Bakshi brothers. These photographs were put in a pamphlet that was used by G M Sadiq's DNC against their rival Bakshi Ghulam Mohammad.

—Arvind Gigoo

Getting tied to formal education was not his cup of tea but he mastered the art of writing English to such an extent that he could beat any highly educated journalist or writer. His interviews had a clear perspective. I was an admirer of his analysis.

—Hriday Nath Jattu

LILTING MUSIC & JAIJAIWANTI

'I WAS MARRIED on 17 July and on the morning of the eighteenth, I was sent to Bansi Parimu's Barzulla house. Being the last child of my parents, my marriage was a week-long celebration and feasts were served to guests for seven consecutive days', recalls Jaya Parimu, or Jaijaiwanti, Bansi's wife. The families were friends and relations, and the alliance between them was arranged and they had met.

Jaijaiwanti's father, Pandit Ved Lal Dhar, was a revolutionary, who, in his youth, had set an example in the orthodox Kashmiri Pandit community by marrying a widow. By words and deeds, he was liberal and a progressive person. He had three daughters and a son. He ensured the best possible education for his children. He was a gifted musician with profound knowledge of the Hindustani classical and Kashmiri Sufiana music.

Pandit Ved Lal was also a pioneer of Kashmir's theatre movement. During his youth, Pandit Ved Lal had stayed at Kolkata for three years where he joined the Alfred Theatre Company and developed friendship with well-known actor and singer, Kundan Lal Saigal.

Pandit Ved Lal Dhar (1899-1978) lived in Srinagar city and owned orchards and sizeable agricultural land in Kashmir. He had named his two daughters Jaijaiwanti and Rageshwari. These are names of Ragaas in Hindustani classical music. Rajkumari, the third daughter, was the most talented of the three sisters. She was a vocalist, a radio artist, and a stage performer. She was the youngest and died very young in

1964. Their brother Vishwapran Dhar did his PhD from IIT Mumbai and taught at the Regional Engineering College (now NIT), Srinagar. He was a classical singer and a harmonium player who had perfect knowledge of Hindustani classical music and the Ragaas. He was also an approved A grade artist of AIR and also the music Guru to well-known singer Vijay Malla.

Quite often, impromptu music programmes were held during the get-together functions at the family's Zaindar Mohalla house. During these hurriedly arranged programmes, Rageshwari would sing while Jaya and Vishwapran would play on the tabla and harmonium respectively. Pandit Ved Lal would also be present and watch his children perform to perfection. The Gazal singer Begum Akhtar had cordial relations with Pandit Ved Lal Dhar's family. Quite often, Begum Akhtar sought Rageshwari's vocal support in her concerts.

In his book, *Radio Kashmir And My Days In Broadcasting*, Pran Kishore Kaul writes:

> Probably the first student of Indian classical music (in Kashmir) was Rageshwari Dhar Mattoo, followed by her sister Jaijaiwanti Dhar Parimu. The talent of both the sisters had been discovered by their father, the social rebel and the activist, Pandit Ved Lal Dhar Vakil in their childhood. Pandit Ved Lalji was one of the earliest classical singers of Kashmir, who joined Radio Kashmir as a long-term casual artist only in the sixties. Rageshwari had a very soft and melodious voice. I recorded the Vaakhs of Lalleshwari, translated into Hindi by Dr Shashi Shekhar Toshakhani, in her voice for the National Programme of Classics on Lal Ded, jointly written by Prof Jay Lal Kaul and me, for which, the Kashmiri Vaakhs were rendered by Raj Begum. Another contribution by Pandit Ved Lal was in training his son, who by profession although an engineer, continued broadcasting till the exodus of Kashmiri Pandits from Kashmir. He was a good Gazal singer.

There were night-long music *mehfils* in Pandit Ved Lal's house at

Zaindar Mohalla. Many renowned musicians performed in these mehfils. In the book, *Master Musicians* of India, under the chapter, 'Sabri Khan', Ustad Sabri Khan (the sarangi player) says that one day he performed at Pandit Ved Lal's Srinagar house till 5 am, playing Darbari for two hours. About these music *mehfils,* Moti Lal Kemu writes:

> I used to reside at Tankipora locality in Srinagar city close to the house of Pandit Ved Lal Dhar. Pandiṭ Dhar was a connoisseur of Hindustani classical music. Many times I saw Begum Akhtar coming to Pandit Ved Lal's house during evening time. There were singing sessions till the late hours of the night. Jaijaiwanti and Rageshwari, the two daughters of Pandit Ved Lal, would also join Begum Akhtar in these singing sessions. During Begum Akhtar's stage performance, Rageshwari would be seen accompanying her by playing on a tanpura. Rageshwari considered herself a disciple of Begum Akhtar.

Bansi Parimu's brother, who served in the Indian Air Force, was married in this Dhar family to a niece of Pandit Ved Lal. Bansi Parimu was, therefore, a frequent visitor to Ved Lal's house. Pandit Ved Lal Dhar had also seen young Bansi Parimu painting background scenes or creating sets for some plays of the theatre groups he patronised. Bansi Parimu had never shown any direct interest in Jaijaiwanti. Parimu was close to a girl, but the affair didn't last long. After this, he got involved with another girl who worked for Radio Kashmir, but this too did not last long.

Jaijaiwanti, or Jaya as she came to be known after her marriage, was a smiling, pretty, sharp and intelligent girl. She had done her post-graduation in music and sociology from the Gandharva Sangeet Mahavidyalaya, Mumbai and Lucknow University respectively. She had also done her B Ed from the Kashmir University in 1965. She was a lover of music and fine arts. She was aware of Bansi Parimu's artistic activities as well as his failed relationships, when she met him formally. By this time Parimu had made a name for himself.

He had also built an independent house at Sanatnagar in Barzulla that he named Takhleeq (Creation). He later purchased the adjacent house, that originally belonged to his sister, and named it Tassavur (Imagination). He was a self-taught artist. Parimu had not attended college after his schooling. He was about nine years older to Jaijaiwanti. Age and educational mismatch did not seem to matter for a progressive person like Pandit Ved Lal, who had seen the spark of talent in young Bansi Parimu.

Those days, marriages were a daytime affairs and food was served to Baratis or close family members and relations only. Friends and colleagues were invited to a tea party in the marriage function celebrated by the bridegroom's family. The tea party was held at Parimu's Barzulla house. Nothing like present-day reception lunches could be imagined in those days due to the financial constraints in the lower-middle-class Pandit families. Capt S K Tikoo, a close family friend, says that Bansi Parimu brought about some changes in his tea party. He added kebabs, a luxury those days. That day, many people came uninvited to greet Parimu and see the bride. Jaya Parimu says, 'Most of the guests came to Barzulla uninvited. Out of curiosity, they wanted to see their friend settled in life. It was very hot, and Pandit Shambhu Nath Alkausar, who was running a shop at Amirakadal in Srinagar, brought many crates of Sharbat-e-Rooh-Afza for the reception. He was a senior cousin by adoption to Bansi and loved him more than his biological cousins. His joy knew no bounds once he came to know about Bansi's marriage and was very happy to see Bansi settled. He was a close relation and a great man whom I held in high esteem'.

After the marriage, Jaijaiwanti got busy with her job as a music teacher in a local college and Bansi focused on his work. The couple struck a good understanding.

Bansi, a liberal non-interfering man, needed space for his artistic pursuits. Jaijaiwanti understood these requisites and demands and provided him with ample space for his creative outpourings. 'So the wild horse has been finally tamed', is what D P Dhar is reported to have told Jaijaiwanti when he saw the couple after their marriage.

The couple had two daughters, Jheelaf and Chandrika. They inherited their love for music and art from their parents. Bansi loved his daughters intensely. He wanted them to do something outstanding in their lives. He did not live to see them getting married and settled. The girls did their schooling from the Presentation Convent School in Srinagar and later studied in New Delhi and Mumbai. Jheelaf lives in Canada while Chandrika is settled in Connecticut (USA) . Both are happily married.

A LOVING HUSBAND, AN AFFECTIONATE FATHER

Remembering her husband, Jaya Parimu says:

> He was a doting husband even while being busy with his own work and engagements. Whenever my official duties demanded my presence as head of some college troupe on tour within or outside the State or country, he was the first person to support and encourage me. I had much reservation on account of the children and family. 'We will manage, don't miss it' was his immediate response. He had a different attitude towards money. For days he could live without even a penny in his pocket and on any day, if he felt he needed to spend and he had money with him, he would spend even ten or twenty thousand rupees. Never did he change his basic principles for pecuniary gains. Never did he borrow from friends or relations or any person. He was always a giver.
>
> After the migration of Pandits from the valley in 1990, I was posted at a Camp College in Jammu, so I could not join him when he decided to shift to Delhi. My eldest daughter joined him as she had to go for some good college education. I was always worried about his health. He had arthritis and diabetes. Before he left for Delhi, I told him, 'You set up a studio here. We will stay under one roof. I am worried about your health'. To this, he said, 'I am quite fit and fine. What shall I do in Jammu? Jammu is presently preoccupied with many issues relating to the colossal

human tragedy of the migration of natives from the Kashmir valley. In Jammu, I get shocks when I see our elderly women living in tents under the blazing sun. Delhi is a metropolitan city where our daughter will get some good education. Here schools and colleges are crowded due to the sudden influx of Pandits from Kashmir. And then how far is Delhi? It is a night's train journey. We have an instant telephonic link. You take care of your job and Chandrika. That is more important'.

He was fond of flowers. He knew much about many varieties of flowers. He grew a variety of flowers in our Sanatnagar, Barzulla House. It was real happiness to watch colourful flowers all around. Dutch tulips, marigolds, roses, narcissus, and many other flowers. This hobby made him and our family happy. We spent many happy evenings together, watching those colourful flowers in full bloom. It was all his creation. He had planted fruit trees and a Chinar tree. Grafting was practised by him in our garden. This technique he had learned from some gardener and mastered it. The Chinar was a symbol of culture for him. He was emotionally attached to the Chinar tree. He gifted many flowerpots to his friends. I remember him gifting one such pot to his friend Shafi Shaida. He was interested in pottery also.

He loved the poetry of Faiz, Jigar and Sahir. Iqbal Bano was his favourite Gazal singer. He liked everything that Iqbal Bano sang. Poems like *'Zard paton ka ban jo mera des hai'*, *'Hum Dekhenge-Laazim hai ki hum bhi dekhnege'* and *'Meray dil meray mussafir'* written by Faiz Ahmed Faiz remained his favourites. Talat Mehmood remained his lifelong favourite. A cup of coffee or Kashmiri Kahwa, some music and he got busy painting in his studio. He had a large collection of classical music, mostly instrumental. Ravi Shanker, Panna Lal Gosh and Ali Akbar Khan were his favourites. He would generally sleep at 2 am. He read a lot and subscribed to some magazines like Life, Reader's Digest, India Today, Sunday and Time. Listening to BBC news was a must for him every morning, before moving out of the bed. Sometimes during late evenings, he would play some tune on a flute. He loved to play upon the flute. He had collected a variety of flutes. He visited the Amarnath cave at least seven times. He had also painted the cave or the abode of Shiva.

Jheelaf Parimu Razdan, Bansi Parimu's daughter, says:

My father was an extremely liberal and unconventional human being. He was a free thinker, born ahead of his time. I feel Kashmir was not ready for him; even India was also not ready for him. Perhaps, he was born in the wrong place at the wrong time. Despite all his achievements in a short span of time, he died unsung. He died for Kashmir and his love for his homeland was incomprehensible and obsessive. Whilst the world thought that painting was his first love, I believe Kashmir was his only love and everything else was peripheral.

As a father, he was not overprotective. He was extremely affectionate but had a temper as well. He would not sermonise, impose or intimidate – he would simply be supportive, watch me make mistakes from a distance and encourage me to move out of my comfort zone. I was faint-hearted, and he constantly pushed me to be strong. He did not understand discrimination, never treated me like the weaker sex as he was not oriented that way. I don't think I would be able to match his determination and will power. He had seen many hardships from a very young age, perhaps that made him strong and kept him grounded as well.

If I were to view him from an outsider's lens and not as a daughter, I would say he was multifaceted, talented and inspiring. I particularly admired him for his social skills, knowledge, integrity, and compassion. He was a great artist but also had a passion for journalism, politics and environmental issues. His political ideology was communism and in his early years, he was an activist with strong views on economic exploitation and capitalism. He was self-taught and found his calling at a young age. Pursuing his passion didn't come without challenges and obstacles but with very little support and encouragement, he overcame them and became what he wanted to be.

I have vivid memories of attending his exhibitions right from the age of three, watching him paint in his studio in Kashmir, having artists of repute come home, visiting art galleries, making amateur attempts under his supervision. When he painted, he was completely engrossed in it. It was perhaps therapeutic for him. It was his opium and his reverence. Even his frail health would not stop him from painting continuously for hours without respite.

My father loved nature and flowers. He built a very pretty hut-like home for himself where I was born. He raised and nurtured one of the most beautiful gardens in Srinagar. He loved gardening. Our garden had a variety of flowers like roses, tulips, chrysanthemums, gerberas, daffodils, narcissus, hyacinths, peonies, and many others.

My father was a unique Kashmiri Pandit. He named his house Takhleeq, and never prayed in his life yet made a painting of goddess Sharika that even the worst period of the turmoil could not dislodge from its place in the iconic Hari Parbat. That's just one of his many contributions to the history of Kashmir.

I don't think I can summarise my father in a few words or sentences. There is so much to be added. He had a great sense of humour and comic timing. He entertained people. He was very extraordinary yet very simple.

Chandrika J P, Bansi Parimu's younger daughter, recalls:

When I look back at whatever little time I got to spend with my father, I find many memories etched in my mind; trips to the India Coffee House, Botanical Gardens in Srinagar and the

Arts Emporium, Srinagar. The visits to the Jehangir Art Gallery and the Dhoomimal Art Gallery weren't mere excursions for me. Today I realise that these trips shaped a larger part of the person that I am today. These were opportunities for me to learn about politics, environmental concerns, gardening, flower arrangement and appreciation of the arts. Even when I was as young as seven years old, my father talked to me about everything under the sun. He helped me to understand these subjects.

His art reflects his skill as well as his passion. He locked himself in his studio for days to paint relentlessly. And the outcome of the days of hard work would be a breathtaking piece of art with the most vibrant and lively colours. He didn't give a title to his abstracts because he enjoyed receiving the diverse interpretations from viewers.

He was not a conventional father, he was a friend to both his children. I remember I could talk to him about anything and get a comforting response every time. He always supported and encouraged me to participate in art competitions and flower shows. He encouraged me to draw and paint Kashmir only. If I ever made something that did not depict Kashmir, he asked me to change it. And he always told me that Kashmir offered plenty of inspiration for creativity.

My father was deeply passionate about gardening. He would himself organise the rows of flowers, the flower beds, and the potted plants. I take pride in saying that our garden had one of the most exotic collections of beautiful flowers. He did not hire a gardener for maintaining our garden. He wouldn't trust anyone with his precious flower collection. We also had a big kitchen garden where he grew collard-greens (Haak in Kashmiri), Kohlrabi (Monji in Kashmiri), French beans, pumpkins, mint, celery, asparagus, chilli peppers, etc. We also had many fruit trees that bore pears, apples, figs, and peaches.

My father was a very social and gregarious person by nature.

One could see him talking to everyone and cracking jokes with people, irrespective of their status. For him, the bus driver or the university professor or the defence minister of India were all human beings. He talked to each with equal enthusiasm. He had a very good sense of humour and he used it as satire for all the social and environmental causes that he supported. He was a voracious reader and enjoyed reading about art, plants, animals, history, architecture, photography etc. I have known my father as a very hardworking man with simple needs and high thinking. He never allowed hatred, malice, and greed to come near him. His homeland was his joy and his source of strength.

COMPASSIONATE HUMAN BEING, A DEPENDABLE FRIEND

Sab ka madaawa kar daala, apna hi madaawa kar na sakay.
Sab ke to girebaan see daale ,apna hi girebaan bhool gayay

To everyone's problem,
I found a solution,
However, for my troubles,
I had none.
I stitched everyone's tattered apparel
but forgot my own torn dress.

—Majaz Lakhnavi

Helping friends and relatives without letting anybody know was a special feature of Bansi Parimu's personality. This help came in different ways and was quite often financial. His own family would come to know about it by accident. He never entertained any discussion on such issues.

'He was a clean man, silent helper, and a compassionate human being. His integrity was crystal clear. His heart was free from any malice. Such sincere and loving human beings are god's gift to this world', says M K Tikoo.

Many people told me several interesting stories about Bansi Parimu's compassion and humane nature. One common trait of his personality that surfaced was his helpful attitude to people who came in contact with him. He rendered assistance to all irrespective of caste, creed, colour or religion. Many among the needy and the poor got appointed as daily wagers through his recommendatory slips and finally got regularised in government jobs. Jaya Parimu has this story to tell, "a theft by a servant in our family was ignored and overlooked by him with one line, 'forget about it, the poor boy must have needed money."'

He had many friends within the State and outside. 'Many names come to my mind who were just like our extended family', recalls Jaya. Shamim Ahmed Shamim was like a brother to him. In Delhi, he became a close friend of V M Tiwari who retired as Air Vice Marshal. Tiwari has authored many books and articles on diverse subjects like birds, travel, Upanishads, electronic warfare, poetry and meditation. He was close to the cinematographer and photographer, Vijay Hangal, son of noted actor A K Hangal, adds Jaya Parimu.

'My father-in-law always said innocently that "Bansi has taken a secret oath not to reveal how and when he helps others". The mason who built our house, the gardener and the milk seller would always come to him with their problems. These problems were about the schooling of their children, employment, opening of bank accounts and financial help. A group of Namda workers once approached him when we were in Kashmir and he helped them by pleading their case. We don't know what their plea was but after his death, a few of them met me in Jammu and confided that their livelihood was saved because of his help and intervention. These Namda-makers said that if he had passed away in Kashmir, they would have come out in thousands for his funeral. I still don't know what he had done for them. He never mentioned these things', Jaya recalls.

> I did my two-year diploma in commercial art from New Delhi. Jammu was hot and unbearable. I wanted to set up some business in Srinagar. In the fifties, I opened a commercial art shop at Red

Cross Road, Srinagar behind the KMDA bus stand. Suraj Tiku and G R Santosh were my friends. Both were fantastic commercial painters apart from being seasoned in fine art. Tiku could work on larger-than-life hoardings. I was frequently interacting with Mohan Raina and Bansi Parimu and many other artists from the Kashmir valley. Parimu was a great help. Though I had no dearth of work, yet at times I needed some guidance to finish the contractual obligation of many departments. At that time, Parimu was young yet very sharp and his mind had many options for solving any problem. I did not see this unique quality in many artists whom I met. He had a heart of gold. For some typical issues, I listened to the suggestions from all but it was Bansi Parimu's guidance that appeared feasible and I implemented what he suggested. I came to know that he died very young. Very unfortunate.

—Sardar Santokh Singh

Pioneer in the field of commercial art in J&K

Bansi Parimu was god's gift to the people of Kashmir. He never believed in divisive or communal politics. Even as a sufferer or a migrant, never did he change his firmly rooted convictions in these matters. His heart throbbed with compassion and empathy for the common man. His concerns had a broader canvas. He worked for the preservation and protection of the living and non-living things of his Kashmir. His mind was ever busy in that pursuit. His concern was the preservation of tradition, culture, and heritage. He was ahead of his time. Had he lived and had there been no painful events in Kashmir, he would have made a significant contribution towards the environmental and ecological issues that we face today. He was a Kashmiri to the core. Militancy gave him a big jolt and cut short his life. And one thing more, we have never been fair to our genuine icons.

—Farooq Nazki

a noted Kashmiri poet and broadcaster

I got to know Bansi Parimu during my university days and the association lasted till he left Srinagar in the early '90s. Being neighbours, we often met at his house. Such a gentleman and such an end! The more I think of him, the more I realise his varied interests. He was a multidimensional personality in the true sense of the word and above all, an extremely good human being. I saw him one day before he migrated. I searched for him in that abandoned house until it was purchased by someone else. It is really painful to recollect the trauma we all have gone through.

—Abdul Majeed Baba

businessman, and a friend of Bansi Parimu

For me, he was like a Guru. Long back, I met him in the Middle East, perhaps in Dubai. He was intense in everything that he did. Intense for any cause and intense with colours. Always brilliant with colours and in conversation. Had he lived, he would have done wonders (*zinda rehtay to kamaal kartay*). Unfortunately, he came to Delhi in very bad shape when he had been uprooted from his homeland. Had it been in the sixties or seventies, he would have been among the top names in the world of art. He was politically aware and very much concerned about Kashmir that was close to his heart.

—Kashmiri Khosa

noted artist

He was impartial and for him, there was hardly any difference between a Pandit and a Muslim. If he could do what he was capable of doing, Bansi would never hesitate. I will not make certain things public but let me tell you that Bansi Parimu has helped many people to get jobs, to get admission and guided them as to what they should learn in art and where they should go. I have personally taken many boys to him and sought his help. He was a silent helper.

—Hriday Nath Jattu

President, All India Kashmiri Pandit Conference

The sculptor Rajendra Tiku recalls:

> He was a rebel. He was very senior to me. Looking at him, many persons like me thought of art as a serious profession. That way he was a great inspiration. As a young boy, I vividly remember him addressing a gathering outside the United Nations Military Observer's office at Gupkar Road, against Israeli attacks on Palestinians. He spoke clearly and boldly on the issue. Migration from Kashmir had hit him hard. In Delhi, he was more agitated by insensitivity and apathy of the bureaucracy and politicians. He was against communalism of any type coming from any quarter. He joined the demonstration 'Artists against Communalism' in Delhi after the killing of Safdar Hashmi. On that day, he also wanted to speak but the organisers didn't allow. He immediately moved out on the road and hung some posters around his neck to draw the attention of the people towards the problems being faced by the victims of terrorism in the Kashmir valley. He stood at the road for the full day and drew the attention of the pedestrian crowds, intellectuals and journalists.

'Bansi Parimu was untouched by materialistic ambition or greed. He was fired by his zest to be a good human being and good artist. And, fortunately for him and for his friends and admirers, he eventually turned to be both. It was in the '50s that we met, at times at his Habba Kadal home. Our association remained intact till his last when both of us had shifted to Delhi in the 1990s. He never liked to wear his personal attributes on his sleeves. He practiced them all through his life. He braved more than his due share of difficulties in life – personal as well as professional, but never showed it. That made him stand out from the crowd', Mohammad Sayeed Malik, a senior journalist, wrote on my facebook post on 20 January 2018.

'Bansi Parimu had many concerns and many issues close to his heart. All of them were meant for the welfare of the common man in Kashmir. He put them before the concerned authorities as and when he got an opportunity. By 'opportunity' I mean in gatherings, public functions or meetings. Many a time, he got up in public functions and put forth his point of view, brushing aside all norms. That was a selfless service to the common man of Kashmir. I have not seen any person in Kashmir who had such courage of conviction. I am privy to the help he rendered to many people, helping them to stand up. A letter of introduction, a telephone call and sometimes accompanying them in person. Any person from any religious background could seek his help', recalls Captain S K Tikoo.

'It is an act of ungratefulness for the establishment that does not recognise his selfless efforts in many fields, other than the promotion of art in the State', Tikoo opines.

The noted artist, Veer Munshi, remembers:

> The moment I decided to go for some training in fine arts in the early seventies, my father took me to Bansi Parimu's house at Sanatnagar, Barzulla in Srinagar. It was an amazing meeting. I was wonderstruck when I saw his studio. He introduced me to Gayoor Sahib who was a well-known sculptor and teacher at Institute of Music and Fine Arts in Srinagar. I was admitted to the evening classes at IMFA, Srinagar and simultaneously I pursued my graduation. It was he who later suggested that I should go to Baroda.
>
> I am indebted to him for showing me the right way at a very critical time in my life. He was like a big brother, a senior comrade and a guide who always sought the welfare of his companions. After the displacement from the Kashmir valley, I met him frequently in Delhi. He never carried any ill will against any person. He would always say 'we', 'our loss', and 'our welfare'. In Delhi, I have never heard him say, I, my, you and your. I have seen him very closely. He would not speak anything even against those who had betrayed him.

The poet and Panun Kashmir leader, Agni Shekhar, recalls, 'Bansi Parimu was an intensely compassionate human being, silent helper for causes close to his heart and a man without malice. He loved everything that had any link with Kashmir. He would not discuss or argue where he felt his intervention may change things for better. "Come, let us go and put it before the man who has to decide this issue". That was his response. That style came from the depths of his heart that had genuine compassion and fellow feelings.

'I was impressed by the sincerity of his feelings. I was impressed not only by his conviction but more by the courage of conviction that he demonstrated', says Agni Shekhar, adding, 'Cobwebs of Apathy or Exodus I or Exodus II that he painted after the displacement of Kashmiri Pandits from the valley are tributes to the struggle of the community in exile. I have written a poem on him. It came out spontaneously from some place within the depths of my heart. I wish he had lived more. After his death, we organised a programme in his memory and instituted an award in his name that came to be known as Bansi Parimu Smriti Sammaan. Ravindra Jamwal, the well-known sculptor from Jammu, was presented the first award. Bansi Parimu's entire family joined that function.

'In January 1991, when Parimu addressed the mammoth gathering of the displaced Pandits in the Gandhi Bhawan auditorium in Jammu, he started with the words, 'Hello fellow sufferers'. One quality that differentiated him from his contemporaries was that he was always a part of the solution. If you presented a problem to him, solutions surfaced in his creative mind immediately. My salute to his wife Jayaji who provided Bansi Parimu with ample space to do what he wanted to do. He was a great human being and a comrade who left us midway in our journey and struggle,' continues Agni Shekhar.

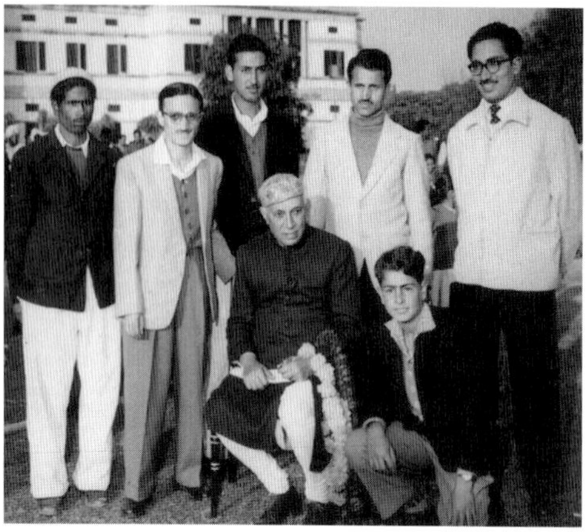

Bansi Parimu with Pandit Jawahar Lal Nehru

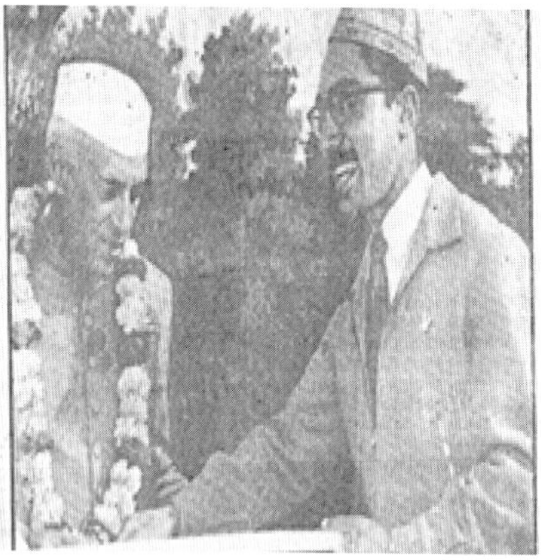

Presenting a painting to Nehru

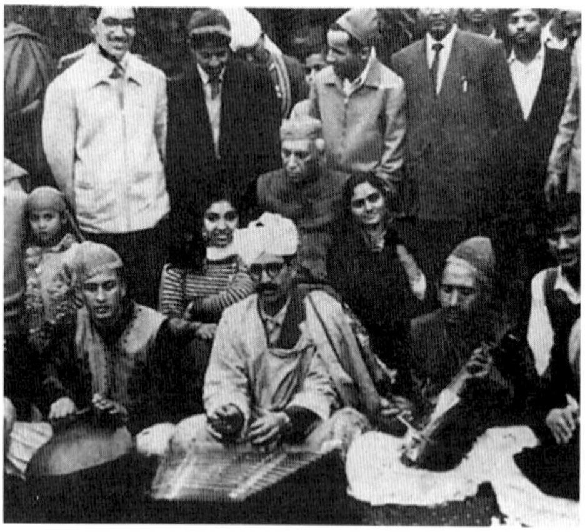

With Nehru and Sufiana artist Tibetbqal

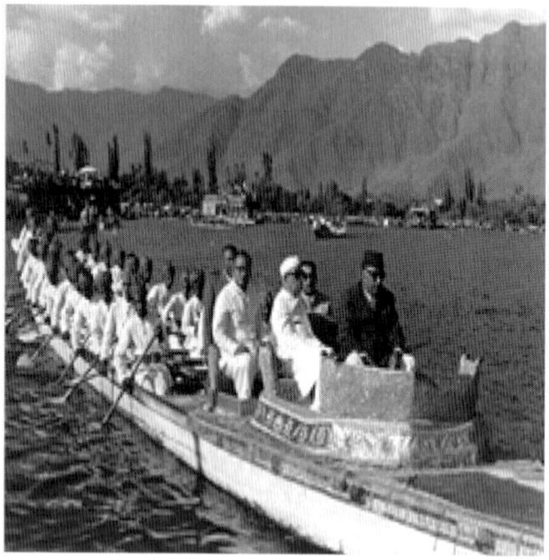

Nehru and Bakshi in Dal Lake, 1956

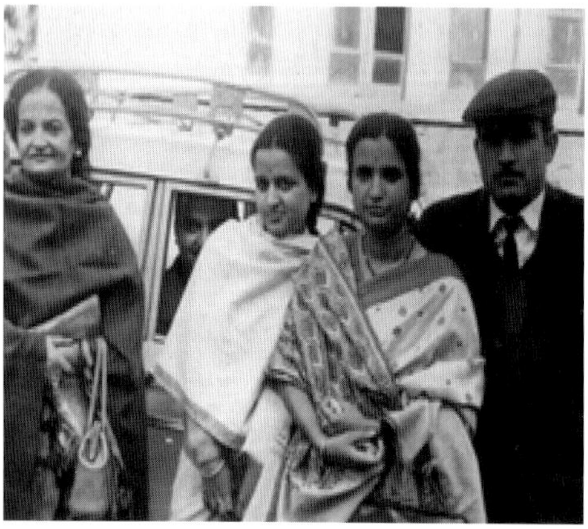

Begum Akhtar with siblings Jaya Parimu, Rageshwari Mattoo and Vishwapran Dhar

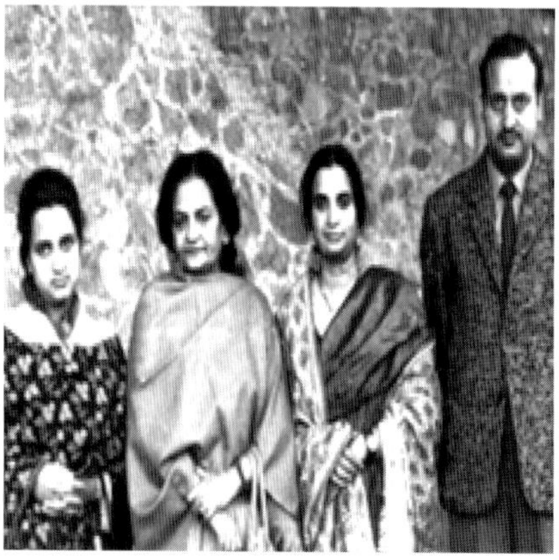

Jaya, her sister Rageshwari and her husband CL Mattoo with Begum Akhtar

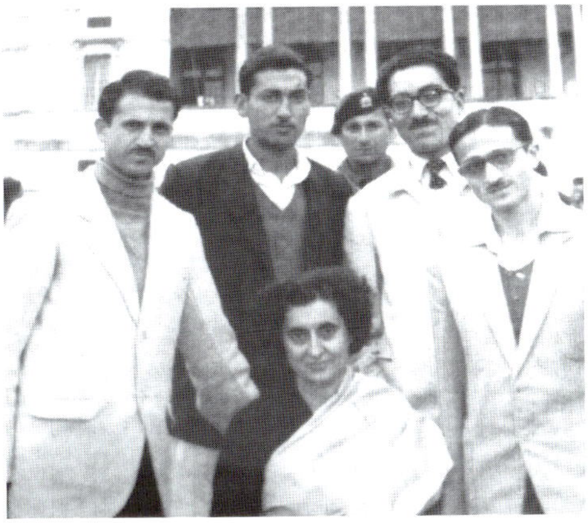

With Indira Gandhi

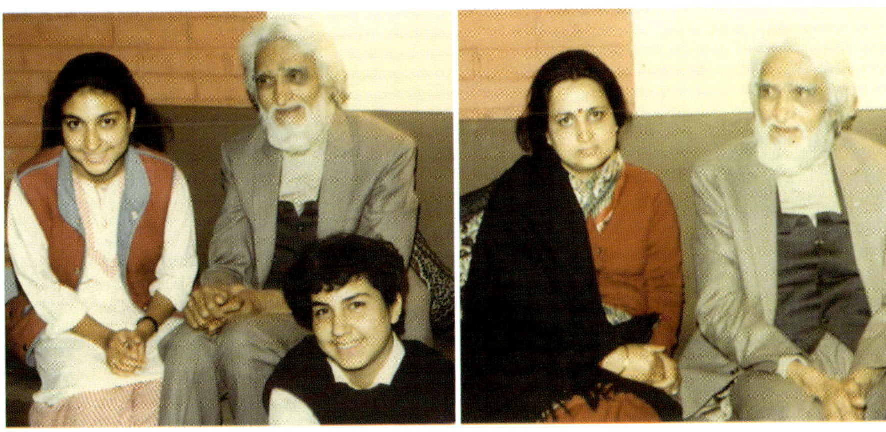

M F Husain with Parimu's daughters; and Jaya at Parimu's house in Srinagar

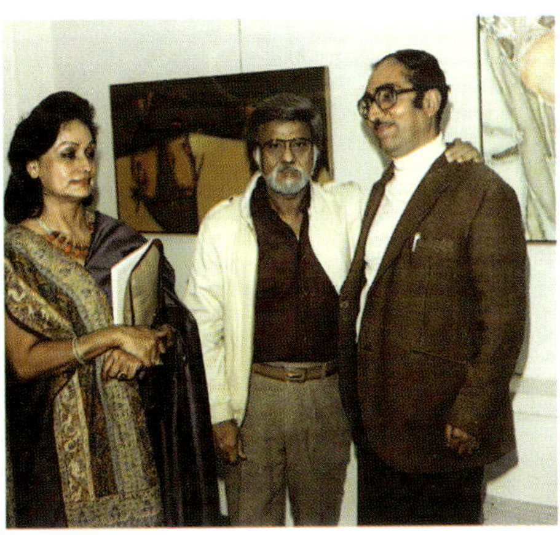

Satish Gujral and his wife at Parimu's exhibition

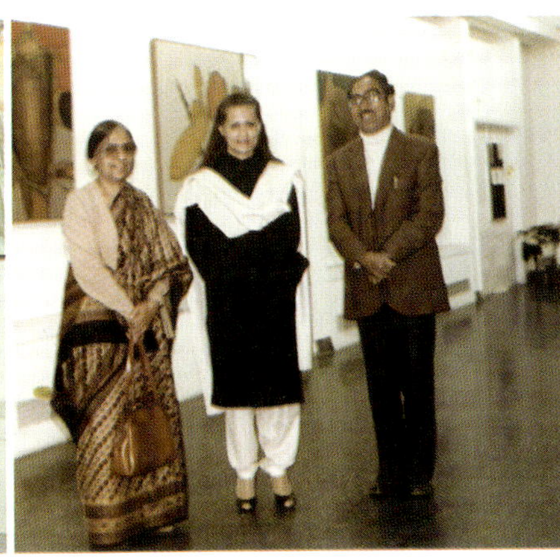

With Sonia Gandhi and Usha Bhaghat

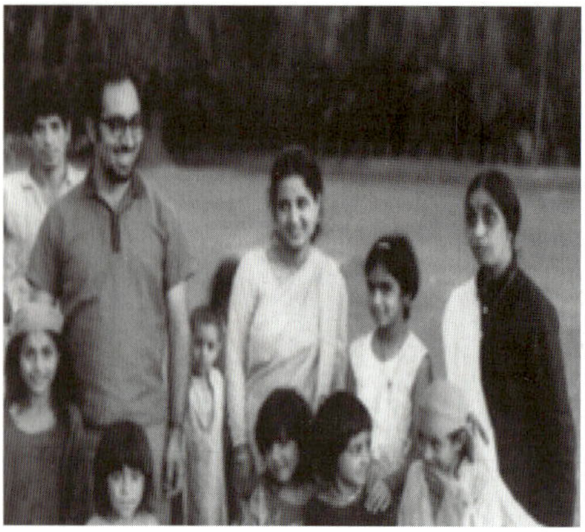

Parimu family with Tyeb Mehta's family at Ganderbal, 1971

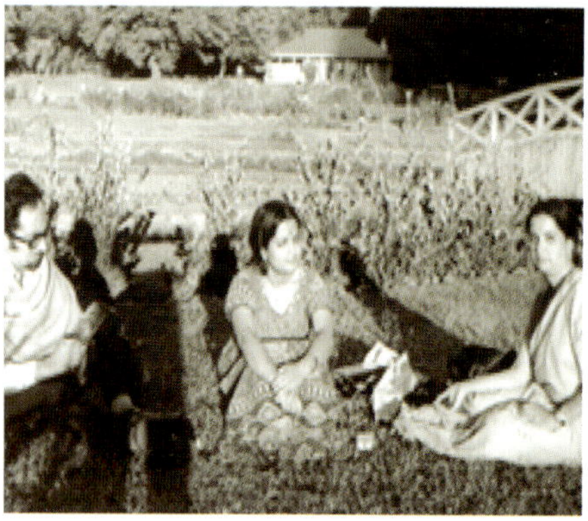

Bansi Parimu, Jaya and Rageshwari

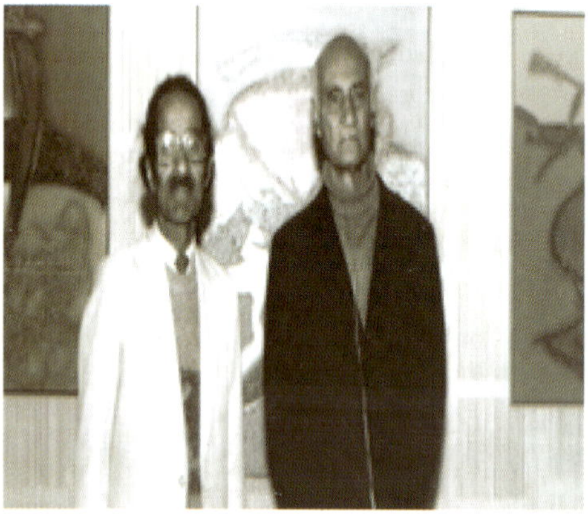

Amin Kamil and Bimal Dasgupta at Bansi Parimu's painting exhibition

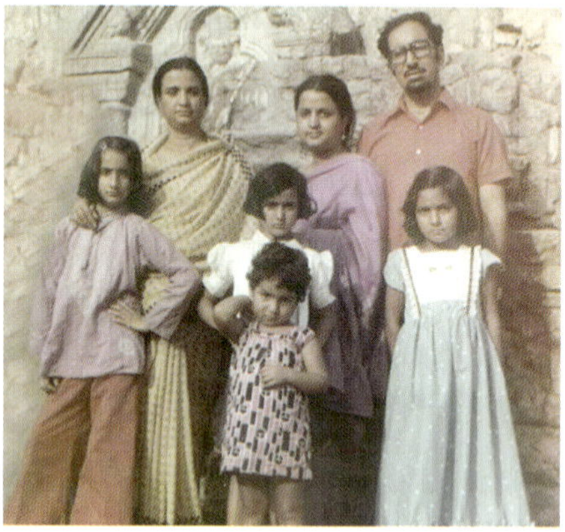

A family picnic

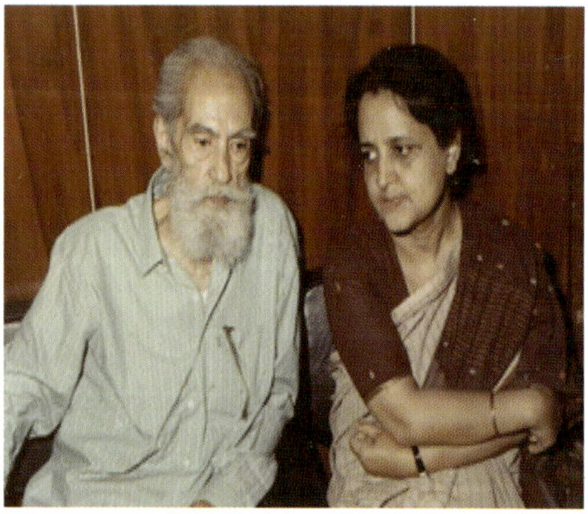

B. C. Sanyal condoles Bansi Parimu's death

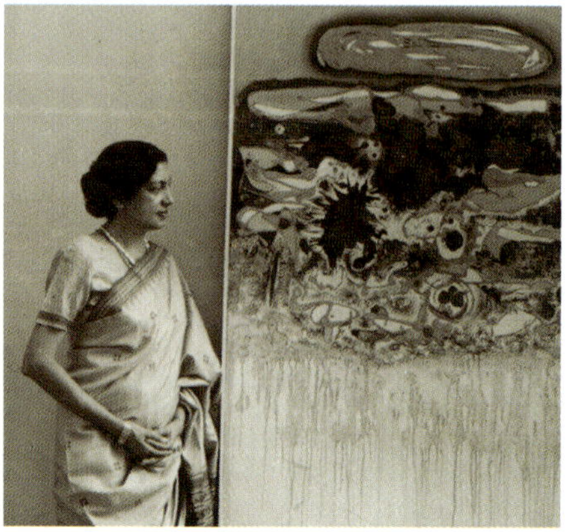

Mrs Ranu Mukerjee buys a Parimu painting

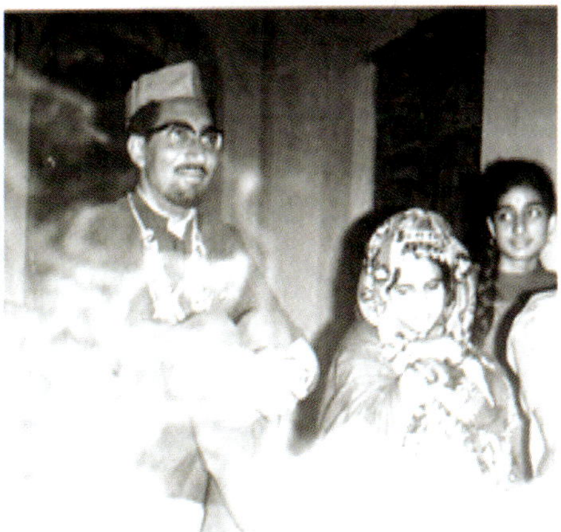

July 17, 1969, Marriage Day, Bansi and Jaya

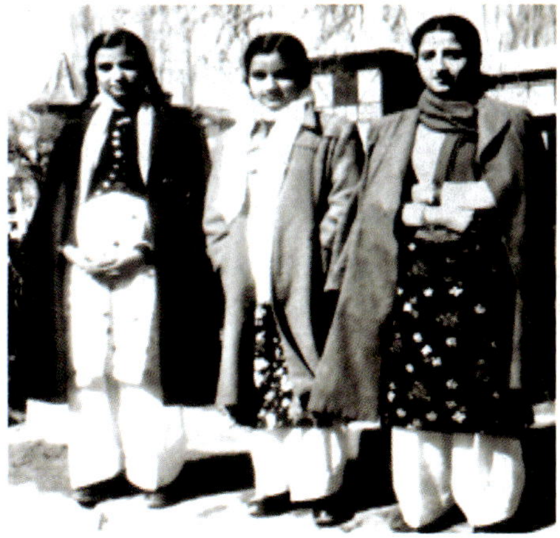

The sisters: Rageshwari, Jaya and Pushpa

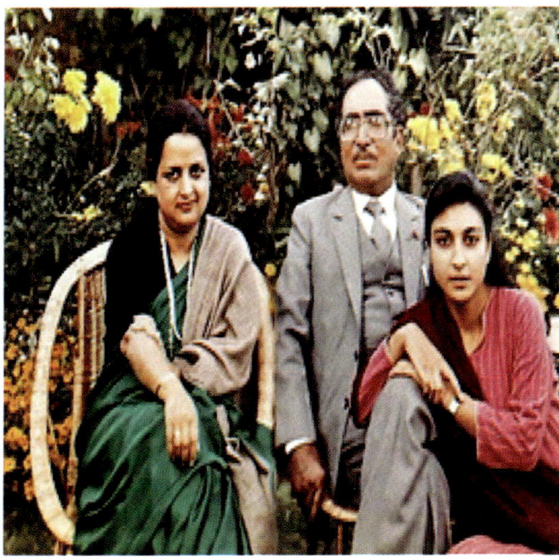

Bansi Parimu with his wife and daughter, 1989

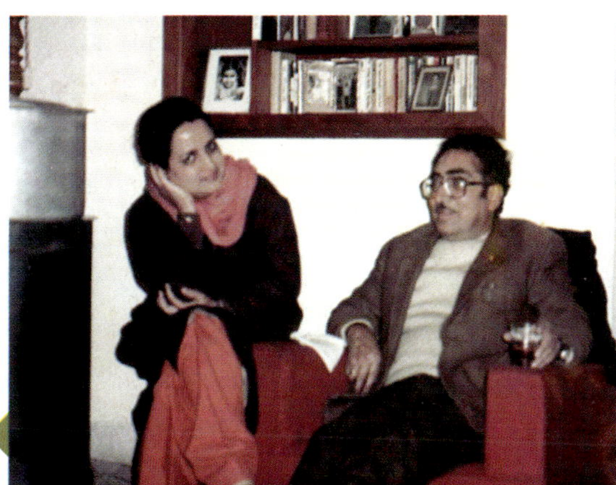

Bansi Parimu and Jaya Parimu, Srinagar 1989

THE LAST DAYS

BANSI PARIMU BELIEVED all that was happening in his beloved Kashmir in the nineties was a temporary phenomenon. He remained in Kashmir even after the terrifying happenings of 19 January, 1990. Though it made him sleepless, yet in his wildest dreams, he could not entertain the idea of leaving Kashmir. With nothing to do, he went out of the valley and held an exhibition of his paintings in New Delhi during February 1990. By June 1990, he had finally made up his mind to live in Delhi, though reluctantly.

In Delhi, Bansi Parimu had many causes, many worries, many involvements that left him with little time to attend to his ailments. Arthritis had already afflicted his hands and fingers. He was diabetic. The hot, humid and hostile climate of the plains too had its adverse impact on him. Although he remained busy in Delhi, yet his life was full of pain and restlessness. His life in Delhi can be best described by the poem, Boat, written by the exiled Kurdish poet, Sherko Bekas. The poem reads:

To me,
my heart is like a boat
with some holes in the bottom.
Again, and again
water presses its way in,
and I bail it out.

Before I have bailed out
a bucketful of old sorrow,
it is already replaced by new sorrow.
But neither does this restless boat sink
nor does it anchor
in the whirlwind of this night.

Talking about Bansi's last years, Jaya Parimu says: 'He didn't like the heat and dust of Delhi. As an artist, he had nothing much to do in Jammu. So, he decided to move to Delhi. Our eldest daughter was admitted to Indraprastha College, for which help came from Moonis Raza's family. After displacement from the valley, some senior bureaucrats from our State, especially Vijay Bakaya, Shafi Pandit and Iqbal Khanday sought Parimu's welfare and were in touch with him. He was also close to Mohammad Shafi Uri. I was still serving in the J&K government. After displacement, I was attached to a camp college in Jammu', Jaya Parimu says. In Delhi, apart from associating himself with fellow sufferers, he was hectic on many fronts, especially his art and journalism. He had started making some good money from journalism and paintings. 'After his death, we received a cheque from the *Times of India* as the balance of payment due to him.'

Before his death, Parimu paid a visit to Jammu and met many friends and relations. He left Jammu on 19 July 1991, after a family picnic to Batote, where he felt cheerful due to the climatic conditions. At Batote, he met Peer Gias-ud-Din who had to leave his home due to armed militancy. 'On 28 July 1991, my daughter Jheelaf suddenly telephoned me and said, "daddy has a gangrene wound and he needs immediate hospitalization". And we rushed to Delhi. He was admitted to AIIMS. On 29 July 1991, he was no more. It was so sudden that I had no time to sit and grieve. He always said to me, "why should I worry about anything when you are around?" With his death, many dreams and plans that he had nourished fell to the ground.'

About the last days of his life, daughter Jheelaf writes:

> My father, in those briefest 12 months of exile, did everything in his power to darn the shreds. He even secured my admission in the prestigious IP College in Delhi University under a 'migrant quota', whereas mother had preferred I study in Jammu. My parents had limited resources but had sensibly invested in a small house on the outskirts of Delhi in Ghaziabad, barring that we had nothing left. A non-Kashmiri friend suggested we name it Swarika - an abode of art and music - my parents were not destined to rebuild nests.
>
> My mother, a professor at the Camp College, continued living in Jammu with my sister who was enrolled in Presentation Convent. I moved with my father to Ghaziabad. We had to share the house with our sympathetic tenant who did not wish to render us homeless all over again. Swarika, however, remained a dream.
>
> My father was even contributing to the formation of 'Panun Kashmir' in its very early days. I am not sure what he was thinking, perhaps he would have steered it in a different direction, had he lived longer. He was possibly going through his *manthan* (churning) at that point. At the same time, he was not losing sight of reality and would often sigh 'the common Kashmiri is now trapped between the security forces and the militants, where will he go?' He was thinking a lot about innumerable issues, but his thoughts and intents of the heart were being usurped by failing instincts for survival.
>
> I was frivolously revelling in my new-found freedom in Delhi, but my father was withering away in melancholy; the shedding leaves of autumn were renouncing the ensuing seasons. Back in Kashmir, I had known him as a fighter who had triumphed bigger battles single-handedly, a rebel, extremely strong-willed and self-respecting, a non-conformist who did not believe in God but certainly in good deeds. Fearing that people's respect

> and adulation for him would instinctively raise expectations from me, at times, I would go into hiding. His imprint was so overpowering. And here I was living with him in exile now, helplessly watching him shrivel and grieve, buried in sorrow, slowly becoming a nonentity. What ailed him?
>
> One sultry evening in Ghaziabad, in his sparsely furnished bedroom cum studio, I saw him seated on his swivel chair facing the easel, gazing at an unfinished painting, his back towards me. I stepped closer to read his pain and then I heard the sobs. That was the first and the last time I saw my father break down. Kashmir was his salvation; clearly, he was choosing it over his young wife and loving daughters.
>
> My mother nonetheless was accommodating, she suggested he return to Kashmir, given his constant pining and yearning. He dismissed the suggestion with, *bu tarre'huh, magar su maahol keti ruud* (I would return but that ambience does not exist anymore), he was anything but bitter. A year of separation appeared like a lifetime to him. On 29 July 1991, he was gone, his galloping gangrene paled before his bleeding heart that perpetually lamented for home.

Jheelaf minces no word in spelling out the varied shades of 'betrayal' that killed him. 'Betrayed by the Indian state, by the institutional silence, by all those he considered his own, those who swore by him, revered him, trusted him, those Coffee House cronies, those aspirants he helped achieve political success without seeking recognition, those he mentored, groomed and supported silently and unconditionally, those who hailed him for his secular credentials. He was heartbroken.' A bullet could not have done worse, adds Jheelaf.

With an unhealed wound of exile, Bansi Parimu fell victim to many secondary health problems that cut short his life. A small, neglected wound on his foot turned gangrenous. Even after amputation, he could not be saved. He was admitted to the AIIMS on 28 July 1991, and he breathed his last within 24 hours. He was just 58 years old at that time and had lived in the national capital for just about a year. Here is the English translation of Agni Shekhar's Hindi poem, *Tum se kaha tha maine*, written on Parimu's death:

I HAD TOLD YOU

I had told you
don't protest
if the Chinar trees are
felled in Kashmir.
Don't say,
our roots,
our mother tongue,
and pitchers full of nectar,
are held by the roots
of these trees.

I had told you,
never speak about
the plunder of our memories,
never oppose the silent change to our historical past.

Don't say that
in the storerooms of our ancestors,
are hidden the guest Mujahideen from Pakistan.
Don't raise your finger
on civil curfews.

I had told you,
don't go alone to Delhi's
Jantar Mantar.
In exile,
don't ever draw paintings of

the cruel and ruthless cobwebs,
wherein,
the victims of
this genocide look helpless.

And then
one day,
silently,
you left for some newer
place,
maybe to India Gate,
to sit for a Dharna
with fists clenched in agony,
wearing weeping and crying posters of our suffering done in
colours.

The sudden demise of Bansi Parimu was a tragedy and a great loss to his wife Jaya and the two daughters. She felt as if life had come to halt on all sides. The education of her children, their careers and finally their marriage were her priorities now. But then she rose to meet many challenges posed by destiny and braved many storms to carry on with her life as best as she could. Jheelaf, recounting the aftermath of her father's death, says:

> My mother turned out to be more resilient and resolute after my father's demise. She kept returning to Kashmir; even courageously witnessed Takhleeq and Tassavur being taken down, to lay the foundation for new homes for the new owners with new hopes. She had made a pact with destiny, *maahol* notwithstanding. She made no claims, she was not going to wait for an invitation, nor seek permission. And to her credit, I got a little closure by visiting Kashmir, after 20 long years. Not many were as fortunate and are waiting even today.
>
> As social media started gaining popularity, once again I became

> privy to innumerable first-hand accounts of Kashmiri Pandits and many facets of our collective tragedy. Consumed by my own survival and misfortunes, I had done nothing for my community, especially the underprivileged, the disconnect became evident. The suffering can never be compared, the humiliation can never be measured, the tragedy can never be underplayed.

His friends have told me that Bansi Parimu used to hum old songs sung by Talat Mehmood. '*Seene mein sulagtein hain armaan.... Taqdeer kahaan le aayi hai*', meaning, 'my heart aches as dreams and unfulfilled desires smoulder within. O fate! where have you brought us?' was one such favourite Talat Mehmood song that he often sang. Jaya Parimu acknowledges, 'Yes, he liked Talat's song, *seene mein sulagtein hain armaan*. The song conveyed his tragedy, pain, and sorrow in exile. He sang it sometime before his death when we went for a family picnic to Batote'. This is how his friends remember their last meeting with Bansi Parimu:

> I was at his bedside when he breathed his last. I flew to Delhi to see him when I came to know about his condition. He was lying unconscious on the bed. One leg had been amputated. A balloon type of thing was to be pressed so that air went to his lungs. His eyes were closed, yet I could see a feeble glow and smile of this dearest friend. It appeared to me as if he was meditating. The doctors told me to keep pressing the balloon and I did so. I found that he breathed only when I pressed. If I stopped, he gasped for ventilation or oxygen. It was all over in a few minutes. That was my Bansi. I am carrying this pain with me. This was the end of a loving person.
>
> **—Capt S K Tikoo**

> It was 1991, and one day I saw Bansi Parimu in the Coffee House at Jammu. He had a camera with him. He sat with us and talked on the prevailing situation. He took many group photographs

of the displaced artists that day. He clicked some Individual photographs as well. I felt as if he was in a great hurry. It looked as if photographing us on that day was a mission for him. And he accomplished it in an hour or so. He developed all those photographs the same day and met me at the Raghunath Bazar, Jammu the next day.

'Bihariji, take these photographs and ensure that every person gets a photo. I have retained my copies. I wanted to hand over the photographs to everybody myself, but I don't know where all of you live. I can't delay it. I have to leave for Delhi and then you don't know what may happen tomorrow. I feel pained to see you here in altogether different circumstances. Please don't get disheartened. A great misfortune has fallen upon us. This won't remain with us forever. It is a cyclone and its nature is to cause death and destruction.'

I received the photographs and did as he wanted me to do. After about ten days I went to Delhi for some work. I wanted to meet Prof Riyaz Punjabi after a long time. He was living in Delhi those days. We didn't have mobile phones at that time so I went to a nearby PCO to speak to Prof Punjabi. And he said, 'Bihariji, you are welcome any time but today I am sad and disturbed. Bansi Parimu is no more. He will be cremated today'. It was very painful news for me. Somehow, I managed to join his cremation that day.

I need to tell you something more. Many people don't know that Bansi Parimu and Prof Muhammad Amin Andrabi were great friends. Nusrat Andrabi, wife of Prof Andrabi, was like a sister to me. That way, I used to call Prof Andrabi as my brother-in-law. Prof Andrabi loved Bansi Parimu and admired his capabilities and sincerity. I have seen them together on many occasions and at many places. Both were good human beings. Prof Andrabi also died young. He must have been sixty or sixty-one years when he died. Parimus and Andrabis had very cordial family relations. Nusrat Andrabi, Jaya Parimu and Hawa Bashir are like sisters. Nighat Hafiz was also close to the Parimu family. After 1990, we lost that bondage and closeness. Never did we think that we belonged to different religions. The idea never came to our minds.

—Bihari Kak

Theatre artist and producer

Recalling his meeting with Bansi Parimu, M K Tikoo says:

Bansi remained a close friend from Sapriyaar, Habba Kadal days. He was like a family member. Just ten days before his death, I was about to board a matador (public transport vehicle) at Jewel Chowk in Jammu when I saw someone's hand on my back. I got down from the footrest of the matador and, to my surprise, I saw Bansi Parimu. He was not cheerful at that time. He held me in a tight embrace, and I asked him to come home. He said, 'no'. He had just returned from Patnitop, Batote and was leaving for Delhi. I said, 'fine, I will see you in Delhi'. I was planning to go to Delhi in a month. He said, 'who knows what may happen tomorrow? Maybe we shall not meet again'. Just after ten or eleven days, I learned that he was no more .I was shocked and his words proved prophetic.

In a Facebook post, Nighat Hafiz wrote:

I remember my last meeting with him and Jaya Parimu at Batote rest house and felt his deep urge and restlessness to visit home. I never thought it was his last trip on the road that led to his half-burnt home in Srinagar, the home that on normal days would bloom with tulips, daffodils, and hyacinths. I also remember how we talked about his paintings, especially the 'Zafran Zaar'. I was a bit uncomfortable with the title he had given, but he convinced me by pinpointing the body-less heads growing on the saffron field painted by him. He must be enjoying the landscapes in paradise.

Talking about Zafran Zaar, Jaya Parimu said, 'The painting was captioned in the posthumous show as Smoldering Crocus and was sold at a much appreciative price to an art collector from Kochi.' Smouldering Crocus was bought by C P Krishnan Nair of 'The Leela Hotels' at a show held in 1992 at Delhi's Dhoomimal Art Gallery.

On Parimu's death, Sabina Sehgal wrote in the *Times of India* of 4 August 1991:

> Parimu will be long remembered for his unstinting support not merely to the cause of art and the artist, but also for his deep association with all the contemporary movements in the State. He was among the very few painters who voluntarily chose to stay in Kashmir despite being isolated from the mainstream, as it were. He never regretted his decision even though he was, in a sense, elbowed out and did not get the national recognition that he truly deserved.

A review of his beliefs and work makes one agree to a clear similarity between Bansi Parimu and the well-known Bulgarian Marxist poet, Nikola Vaptsarov. Both were communists by belief, and both died young. Both were artists, rebels and committed persons. Both died in exile. Vaptsarov produced a series of progressive plays, circulated literature and aroused interest in cultural questions. In early 1941, when the Nazi forces entered Bulgaria and took control of the country as a prelude to the attack on the USSR, Vaptsarov fled to Sofia with his wife and child. Unfortunately, he was arrested by the Nazi forces and punished for his beliefs and convictions. He died on 23 July in 1942, at a young age of 33 years. His poem, History, reinforces the idea of close similarity that Parimu had with this rebel poet. I quote some lines from the poem:

History, will you mention us
in your faded scroll?
For the hardship and affliction
we do not seek rewards,

nor do we want our pictures
in the calendar of years.
Just tell our story simply
to those we shall not see,
tell those who will replace us –
We fought courageously.

The clouds of hate and distrust brought forth by the armed militancy in the Kashmir valley have disfigured faces of all her icons. For sure, these clouds have to dispel one day, and a new dawn has to usher in peace and happiness. At that time, will the Kashmiri society remember its real icons and their contribution? Will history remember them?

Soora phyaakh sapadiethh ta veithi manz bavizem
Be wattan gatchhanuk dinam yena taana lookh.
Krooth raavun tyol ta yaadan hundh alaav,
Kyaa phaban sekilis andher mastaana lookh

When I turn to a handful of ash,
consign me to the river Vitasta,
Lest people ridicule me as an exile from his motherland.
Bitter is the lament of loss and with this din of memories,
How will the carefree people survive in these lifeless deserts?

—Moti Lal Saqi

THE JOURNEY OF ART IN KASHMIR

There can be no mistake about the fertility and verdure of Kashmir; look where you will, everything is green and beautiful, up to the snows which girdle it round – a very garden amongst the hills, an emerald set in crystal – this greenest and loveliest of valleys, which had charmed with its soft and sylvan beauty.

—**Samuel Bourne**[1] (1863-'66)

> I am a lover of Kashmir and all its entrancing beauty, because perhaps, deep down within me and almost forgotten by me, there is something which stirs at the call of the old homeland from whence we came long, long ago; and because I cannot answer that call as I would, I have to content myself with dreams and fantasies, and I revisit the glorious valley girt by the Himalayan snow through books and cold prints. As I write this, my vision is limited by high walls that seem to close upon me and envelop me and the heat of the plains oppresses me.

1 Samuel Bourne (1834-1912), a British traveller cum photographer, undertook three treks to Kashmir and the western Himalayas in 1863, 1864 and 1866, during which he photographed his surroundings extensively. Throughout his travels, he wrote about his first impressions of the places he visited and these writings were published in the British Journal of Photography.

> But Kalhana has enabled me to overstep these walls and forget the summer heat, and to visit that land of the Sun god 'where realising that the land created by his father is unable to bear the heat, the hot rayed sun honours it by bearing himself with softness in summer'; where dawn first appears with a golden radiance on the external snows and, in the evening, 'the daylight renders homage to the peaks of the towering mountains'; where, in the valley below, the lazy sleepy Vitasta winds slowly through smiling fields and richly laden fruit trees, and creeps under the lordly Chinars, and passes through still lakes covered with lotus blooms, and then makes up and rushes down the gorges to the plains of the Punjab below. 'The joy of plunging into the Ganga is not known to those who reside in the sandy deserts', writes Kalhana; how can the dwellers in the plains know the joys of the mountains, and especially of this jewel of Asia, situated in the heart of that mighty continent.
>
> —**Pandit Jawahar Lal Nehru** in his foreword to
> R S Pandit's English translation of Kalhana's *Rajatarangini*

THIS DESCRIPTION IS repeated by many travellers and notable people who visited Kashmir. Its rivers, meadows, hills, snow-capped peaks, lakes, flora and fauna place people into the benevolent lap of mother nature and has been a source of inspiration to many in various creative fields. The mark of this natural beauty has been visible since ancient times in literature, art and the centuries-old cultural heritage of Kashmir.

The *Nilamata Purana* tells us about the existence of sculpture and paintings in ancient Kashmir. This book has many references for the images of Kesava (Vishnu), Sesa, Kamdeva, Brahma, Ananta and Buddha done in stone and metals like copper, brass, silver, and gold. It also confirms that these images were painted on cloth apart from the existence of many Chaityas decorated with paintings. Some verses from the *Nilamata Purana* read:

> In the month of Asaadha, Kesava's (Vishnu's) statue, sleeping on the couch in the form of Sesa, should be made of stone, clay, gold, wood, copper, brass, silver or he may be painted in a picture.
> —**The *Nilamata Purana*** by Ved Kumari Ghai, volume 2, page 109

> Kamdeva painted on a cloth should be worshipped with various types of garlands and diverse incenses on the 13th day bright half of Chaitra.
> —**The *Nilamata Purana*** by Ved Kumari Ghai, volume 2, page 171

It is established beyond any shade of doubt that the fundamental principles of the Shilpa Shastra, Natyashastra and Vastu Shastra were used in the arts and crafts, temple architecture, paintings, sculpture and Hindu iconography in ancient and medieval Kashmir. The influence of *Chitrasutra* and the *Natyashastra* is evident in the paintings and sculptures of Kashmir.

It is believed by many scholars and art historians that the most ancient text on temple construction, paintings and image art known as *Chitrasutra* of the *Vishṇudharmottara Pūraṇa* was compiled by the learned Brahmins of Kashmir. It is the most detailed text on the Hindu iconography of ancient India. This text is a basic guide as to how men and women should be drawn in a painting. For artists, there are clear guidelines listed in the *Chitrasutra* as to how broad features relating to the images of deities, kings and other people should be drawn. We are told:

The *Chitrasutra* text is a basic documented guide as to how men and women should be drawn in a painting. For artists, there are clear guidelines listed in the *Chitrasutra* as to how broad features relating to the images of deities, kings and other people should be drawn. We are told:

1. A female figure should be drawn with one foot calmly advanced, and with the part about the hips and loins broad and flurried on account of amorous dalliance.

2. A painting drawn with care pleasing to the eye, thought out with great intelligence and ingenuity and remarkable by its beauty of execution and charm and refined taste and such other qualities, yields great joy and delight.

Apart from the guidelines detailed in the *Chitrasutra*, artists and sculptors from Kashmir had good knowledge of the Natyashastra. Many available stone or metal sculptures done in Kashmir are based on *Sthayibhava*s and *Rasa*s as explained in the *Natyashastra*. A careful look at the faces, poses, stances and body language of the human figures in sculptures (even in respect of broken sculptures) reveals Sthayibhavas and their corresponding Rasas. In Kashmir, Avantipora Temple sculptures and stone carvings show ample influence of the Natyashastra. Loyalty to guidelines of the Natyashastra is also evident in some terracotta images relating to the 5th and the 6th century CE recovered from Harwan, though most of these precious treasures have moved out from Kashmir and are in the custody of many individuals or museums the world over.

Terracotta tiles relating to a period ranging from the 4th up to the 6th century CE obtained from Harwan are indicators of many key historical facts of ancient Kashmir. The moulded tiles obtained from the excavations of 1925 at Harwan depict designs and images consisting of conventional flowers, combinations of leaves, leaves of lotus plant, ducks, cocks, cows, elephants, deers, archers on horseback chasing a deer, lady carrying a flower vase, a dancing girl, a female musician beating the drum, a soldier in armour, men and women conversing, emaciated Yogis, etc. Each tile has a number in the Kharoshti language that ceased to be in vogue in north-western India, where it had principally flourished, around the 5th century CE.

Abhinavabharati is the most studied commentary on the *Natyashastra*, written by Abhinavagupta (950–1020 CE) of Kashmir, who has referred to the Natyashastra as the Natyaveda. The Shaivite scholar says:

> A creation in art is the expression of a feeling that is freed from localised distinctions; it is the generalisation of a particular feeling. It comes into being through the creative genius (*prathibha*) of the artist. And, it finds its fulfilment in the heart of the viewer, who derives *ananda,* the joy of aesthetic experience. He is, therefore, central to that art-experience. That pleasure must not, however, bind the viewer but must liberate him from his limited confines.

'A true aesthetic object, Abhinavagupta declares, not merely stimulates the senses but also ignites the imagination of the viewer. That experience sets the individual free from the confines of place, time and ego (self). Thus, art is not mundane; it is alaukika, beyond the ordinary', writes the art expert and blogger Sreenivasa Rao.

John Guy, senior curator, the Metropolitan Museum of Art, New York, says:

> The temple sculptures in India, beginning from Kashmir to Deccan, depict dance forms from Bharata Muni's *Natyashastra*. Temples are the places from ancient times which described several dance forms which were practised in that particular area.

A land that gives such a beautiful classic cannot remain ignorant of its actual practice. It is also a fact that some of the greatest contributors to the ancient Indian aesthetics were of Kashmiri origin.

The Burzohama excavations have thrown up many illuminating links for the study of the earliest human settlement in the Kashmir valley. The excavations at Burzohama have revealed pre-historic rock drawings. Pots and pottery excavated at Burzohama have images of animals like the wild goat and long-horned stag.

There is one particular rock drawing at Burzohama that has been established to be about five thousand years old. This artwork shows two bright objects in the sky, with figures of animals and humans. The Scientists believe that this stone drawing at Burzohama is a complete sky chart of the night on which a Supernova was first observed by unknown observers around 4,500 BCE. A supernova is a transient astronomical event that occurs during the last stellar evolutionary stages of a massive star's life, whose dramatic and catastrophic destruction is marked by one final titanic explosion. Thus, using their artistic skills, the inhabitants of Burzohama observed and carved something unique for posterity.

Ancient and early medieval Kashmir has now come to be recognised as one of the most crucial centres in the history of art in entire South Asia. The journey of art, essentially sculptures (brass, bronze and stone), paintings, illustrated manuscripts and wall paintings from Kashmir to Tibet, China and Central Asia is a known fact now. Kashmir's strong links with some parts of Central Asia and Afghanistan in the post-Gupta period have also been established. Kalhana has spoken about many metal sculptures and idols in Kashmir in many verses of his *Rajataringini*. Many brass, bronze and stone sculptures of that period are housed in the SPS Museum in Srinagar, while many can be seen in the museums the world over. Many Bodhisattva figures have been found in the monasteries of Ladakh, Tibet and western Himalayas that can be traced back to Kashmir.

THE BUDDHIST CONNECTION

Tibetan scholar-translator Rinchen Zangpo's biography throws more light on the ancient and medieval interactions held between Kashmir, Tibet, Ladakh, Gilgit, and other places. Zangpo (958-1055 AD) was a contemporary of the scholar Abhinavagupta. This biography tells us that Kashmiri Brahmins brought the art of wall paintings, image and mural-making and cloth paintings to the Himalayas. It was Zangpo who engaged Kashmiri painters to create wall paintings and sculptures in 108 monasteries, of which Alchi in Leh remains a shining surviving example. The commonality of style and form between the available sculptures or painted panels in Kashmir with those in Tibet, Ladakh and some monasteries in the hills of Himachal Pradesh establishes the link conclusively. The earliest illuminated manuscripts available in Tibet bear ample testimony to the Kashmiri styles.

In her book, *The Art of Ancient India: Buddhist, Hindu, Jain*, Susan L Huntington writes:

> Kashmir served as a source of imagery and influence for the northern and eastern movements of Buddhist art. The Yungang caves in China, the wall paintings from several sites in inner Asia, especially Qizil and Tun-huang, the paintings from the cache at Tun-huang, and some iconographic manuscripts from Japan, for example, should be evaluated with Kashmir in mind as a possible source. A full understanding of the transmission of Buddhist art through Asia is dependent on developing a greater knowledge of Kashmiri art.

At the National Museum in New Delhi, I saw a wooden Buddha and a Bodhisattva, probably Maitreya, done in pure Kashmiri Style. It was brought from Khotan. I also saw sculptures, pieces of wall paintings and artifacts at the National Museum that bear evidence of the presence of Kashmiri artists in Dunhuang, Khotan, Miran, Turfan, Astana, Niya and other places which extend from Tibet to Siberia.

The discovery of the wall paintings of Mangnang and Tholing, and the manuscript paintings of Tholing in western Tibet by Giuseppe Tucci marked a real breakthrough in the study of Kashmir's art tradition. Tucci believes that these wall paintings and murals and also the Thangkas are a work of Kashmiri painters done sometime around the 10th or 11th century CE. Similarly, the Tholing Manuscripts were created around the 11th century CE. In terms of subject and style, Mangnang and Tholing can be said to be the pictorial translation of contemporary Kashmiri Bronzes.

The wall paintings and manuscript paintings discovered in western Tibet are now accepted to have been done by painters from Kashmir. These paintings have established clear and unambiguous Kashmiri link of the painters. These paintings bear ample reflection of bronze images of that period in Kashmir, apart from contemporary Kashmiri embroidered costumes with elaborate designs and ornaments.

Carried by sages, savants, scholars, artists, painters and traders from Kashmir, Kashmiri art and artistic trends spread across Asia. The light of Buddhism and its artistic glories, meditational enlightenment and enchanting murals of the cloisters of Kashmir inspired artists to illuminate monastic interiors in the sands of Central Asia, in the snows of Tibet and the sprawling monasteries of China. Along the Silk Route, Kashmir's artistic influence can be seen in the ancient and the medieval period monasteries of the Buddhist faith. This influence is seen in the wall paintings, murals, sculptures and paintings of Bodhisattvas. The eminent Buddhist scholar, Lokesh Chandra, writes:

> The Kashmiri Pandits were not only gifted but they were also equally adventurous. Their adventurous spirit drove them to Central Asia, Tibet, China, Korea, Japan and the Philippines for the dissemination of Indian culture, art and philosophy. In Japan, the *Lotus Sutra* is considered to be the greatest and most popular Sutras of Buddhism today. This Sutra was translated into Chinese in the 4th century by Kumarjiva who was a Kashmiri. A Kashmiri Pandit named Kamalshila was the royal craftsman of the Mongols. Kashmiri Pandits brought the Shilpashastras or canons of creation with them, for which they were given free access to the Mongolian court. A number of Kashmiri Pandits went to Korea. Tyagabhadra, a Kashmiri, and his disciples were responsible there for the choice of the present capital of South Korea – Seol. Yet another gift of the Kashmiri Pandits to Japan is the Siddham calligraphy. There is a tradition in Japan to write Sanskrit Shlokas in a very beautiful script called Siddham. It is a major art in Japan and the Japanese learnt this art from two great Kashmiri Pandits, Prajna and Munishri. Even today there is practically no house where you don't find something written in Siddham.

Apart from artists, Kashmiri scholars and savants have played a leading role in spreading knowledge and Buddhism far and wide across the Himalayan frontiers of India in Central Asia, Tibet, and China. Some Buddhist monasteries in Central Asia had Parmukhs or Pramukhs who were from Kashmir. The Pramukhs were highly respected scholars and polyglots who were proficient in art, religion and philosophy. There were many Buddhist Pramukhs or Parmukhs from Kashmir in Nav-Vihara (a well known ancient Buddhist monastery) of Balkh in Central Asia. During the Arab invasions, some Parmukhs or Pramukhs of Nav-Vihara fled to Khotan and Kashmir, travelling through the Silk Route while many converted to Islam. The Parmukhs of Nav-Vihara were polyglots, who, upon their capture were brought to Iraq by invading Arabs. The services of these Parmukhs were utilised by Abbasid Caliphs for translation of many ancient Sanskrit texts into Arabic. The Parmukhs were paid from the royal treasury of the Abbasid Caliphate for this translation work. The Arabs called them Barmakhs or Barmikahs. They were also known as Barmakids or Barmecides. They were highly influential throughout Arabia, Persia, and Central Asia. Khalid Barmiki became the governor of upper Mesopotamia. Yahaya Barmiki became the governor of Armenia. Al Fadl Barmiki and Jaffar Barmiki occupied key positions during the rule of Harun al-Rashid.

ART IN LADAKH

As in other parts of the world, in Ladakh also, art began with rock carvings. This art, carving can be seen in the different valleys of Ladakh along the Indus, Shayok, Nubra and Suru rivers. One can see this ancient art at places like Taru, Nimmu, Likir, Alchi, Khalsi, Stakna, Karu, Upshi, Kyari and Tangste. For many millennia, hunters, traders and pilgrims have passed through this region and left signs of their cultures and religions. In Ladakh, some rock carvings depicting hunting scenes are reported to be more than five thousand years old. These rock carvings depict dancing scenes, wild animals, sun, moon, stars, mountains, human figures and birds. About four hundred rock carving sites give vital leads about Ladakh's ancient links with Kashmir, Central Asia, Afghanistan and Tibet.

The art of Ladakh is prominently visible in bronze statues, Tibetan dance masks, ritual objects, text scrolls, silks. Thangka paintings and wall paintings (in monasteries). This art represents a tradition that has evolved over many centuries. With the arrival of the Muslim rule in Kashmir from the 14th century, Tibet became Ladakh's only external source of Buddhist learning and art practices. On the artistic front, there is little recorded interaction between Kashmir and Ladakh from the 14th century onwards. Presently, there are many artists in Ladakh who have earned name and fame in the fields of sculpture, Thangka art, wood carving and wall painting. Some prominent names in this category are Tsering Wangdu (a painter awarded Padama Shri), Skarma Tsering (well-known sculptor), Nawang Tsering (well-known sculptor), Tsering Gurmat (trained sculptor), Dorjay Dadul (wood carving), Chimet Rigzin (sculpture) and many more.

ART FROM EMPEROR LALITADITYA AND AVANTIVARMAN'S TIME

Lalitaditya built the Martand Sun Temple in Kashmir on the plateau near Mattan town, in south Kashmir. The location of the temple proves the skill and expertise of Kashmiri artisans of the period. It is said that from this temple, one could see the entire Lidder valley and the demolished Vijeyshawara Temple complex near present-day Bijbihara town.

It is believed that the Martand Sun Temple was decorated with reliefs and paintings. This Sun temple is believed to be the result of the crosscurrents flowing from Roman, Byzantine, Sasanian and late Gupta period. Unfortunately, like many temples, this 8th century marvel faced demolition during the rule of Sultan Sikander Butshikan (1394-1417 AD) of Kashmir. The temple would have been as imposing as the Pyramids of Giza or the Acropolis of Athens, had human hands not joined in its destruction.

Lalitaditya founded the township of Parihaspora on a plateau near Srinagar city. This township had many temples with images of Vishnu, Shiva, and Buddha. According to the verses, 136 to 216 from Taranga fourth of Kalhana's *Rajtarangini*, temples in this township complex had images of Parihaskeshwa, Muktakeshwa, and Goverdhanadhara all done in shining silver and gold. At present, nothing exists in Parihaspora except heaps of broken stones.

Lalitaditya was followed by Avantivarman (855-883 AD). Prosperity visited Kashmir during the rule of King Avantivaraman. He built two temples and gifted them to the Brahmins of Kashmir. Avantiswamin was dedicated to Vishnu while Avantisvara was dedicated to Shiva. Some amazing sculptures were discovered in the excavation of Avantiswamin and Avantisvara temples located on the Srinagar-Jammu highway at Avantipora, a town about 20 km from Srinagar city. Profusely carved sculptures were obtained from Avantiswamin Temple. The temple structures are in a ruined state at present. From scrutiny of stone images excavated at Avantipora, it is clear that Kashmir had achieved a distinct style in sculptural art during the rule of Avantivarman. Both the temples are close to each other.

Ruins of Sugandesh and Sankara Gaurisa temples built by Shankervarman, son of Avantivarman, can also be seen near Pattan on the Srinagar-Baramulla road. By the end of the 11th century, Kashmir's distinct school of art had influenced the entire Himalayan region.

Apart from the SPS Museum, Srinagar and some other museums in the country, the author saw metal (especially brass and bronze) sculptures from Kashmir in many museums of the US. The Metropolitan Museum of Art, New York has some rich collection of stone and metal sculptures from Kashmir. The Rubin Museum of Art located on 17th Street West, New York houses some rare artefacts from ancient and medieval Kashmir, western Himalayas and Tibet. Ivory sculptures from Kashmir were unknown until some such artefacts appeared in various museums of the US and Europe. Apart from ivory, some museums in the US also hold Buddhist and Hindu sculptures from Kashmir done in sandalwood. The ivory and sandalwood sculptures relate mostly to 8th century, done during the rule of illustrious Karkota kings.

PAINTINGS FROM KASHMIR

The journey of painting in Kashmir is well understood from the history of the land. We can summarise it as a journey of four phases: evolution, blossoming, suppression and finally rebirth. The periods could be divided as ancient for evolution, medieval for blossoming, the fourteenth century to the late sixteenth century as a period of suppression and neglect (with the exception of Sultan Zainul Abdin's rule) and finally, the rebirth that started with the arrival of Mughals on the scene.

Kashmir's artistic tradition started facing neglect and suppression from the fourteenth century when Kashmir's throne fell into the hands of the Sultans. Lack of official patronage and religious persecution played a key role in the decline of art during this period. The demolition of temples during the rule of Sultan Sikander Butshikan and, thereafter, played havoc with the artistic treasures of Kashmir. Evidences of old Hindu and Buddhist art were almost erased from the landscape of the Kashmir valley during this period. Many references come up in history books that tell us that there were many temples in the Kashmir valley that had beautiful sculptures, idols, stone carvings and wall paintings. Since almost all temples were demolished and raised to the ground, no visible proof exists anywhere. This period can be called as the dark period for visual arts in Kashmir.

No reference worth mentioning can be found in the books of history or on the ground regarding any mediaeval Sultan of Kashmir encouraging art and sculpture except, of course, the illustrious Sultan Zainul Abdin (1395-1470), when his patronage got reflected in the traditional arts of Kashmir like shawls[2], walnut wood carving, papier-

2 Shawls from Kashmir (Cashmere shawl) became quite popular and trendy in the aristocratic families of France and England. Even Josephine Bonaparte (Napoleon's wife) wore a 'Cashmere Pashmina Shawl'. Josephine Bonaparte had a collection of 60 Kashmiri Pashmina shawls. Emperor Akbar and Ottoman royals also wore Kashmiri shawls that had artistic patterns and designs.

mâché work, carpet weaving, Namda-making and copper Naqqashi. We find some references to paintings in history books during the rule of Sultan Zainul Abdin. Mulla Jamil, his court musician, was also a famous royal painter.

ART DURING MUGHAL RULE IN KASHMIR

About Kashmir's Muslim art, the story of handicrafts, carpet weaving, papier mache art, walnut wood carving, etc. that had been patronized by Sultan Zain ul Abdin, is almost similar due to political unrest and turmoil after his death. This art got a fresh lease of life after the Mughals conquered Kashmir.

It appears that Kashmiri artists picked up the brush again when Mughals appeared on the scene. Mughal rulers, upon their visit to the Kashmir valley, brought many Darbar painters along with them. They painted in the Valley and prepared illuminated and illustrated manuscripts in Persian. Their interaction with local artists is not recorded anywhere though many books inform us that Akbar, Jehangir and Shahjahan had many artists from Kashmir in their courts. Some prominent names in this category are Muhammad Hussain Zarin Qalam, Zainul Abdin, Kamal Kashmiri, Haider Kashmiri, Daud Kashmiri, Salih Kashmiri, and Yaqoob Kashmiri. There were some Kashmiri artists in the court of Jehangir.

After the Mughal rule or the revival phase, paintings done in Kashmir or outside Kashmir by Kashmiri artists can be seen in the illustrated-illuminated religious manuscripts in Sharda, Gurmukhi, Persian, and Sanskrit. These manuscripts, like the *Ramayana, Mahabharata, Guru Granth Sahib, Shiv Puran, Bhagwat Puran* and many more relate to Hindu and Sikh faiths. These paintings can also be seen in the illustrated/ illuminated manuscripts of Hafiz, Sheikh Saadi, Khamsa of Nizami and many other Persian texts. Paintings in all these manuscripts have been attributed to the Kashmiri painters and scribes who lived within or outside the Kashmir valley. These paintings are also seen in the old horoscope scrolls of Kashmiri Pandits. Kashmiri miniatures were bordered with decorative motifs and patterns that usually formed the frame of the main subject.

Broadly speaking, some key features of Kashmiri paintings are:

a) It is a fusion of many styles. Traces of Mughal elements with a Pahari essence is visible.
b) The paintings have ornamental or floral borders but quite often, the artist does not confine his core work within these borders. He tends to jump out.
c) The artists have a lesser notion of space.
d) The artist's commitment to realism or nature is also not strict.
e) Human figures are small and more stress is on conveying some tale or religious story.
f) The colours used are typical to the Kashmiri palette. Colours like saffron, green, yellow, mauve, and indigo are liberally used.
g) Generally, there is a reluctance to sign in the colophon and the artists have mostly chosen to remain unknown.

It appears that a good number of 'Kashmir Miniature Paintings' created for illustrating some Hindu religious manuscripts were done in an unadventurous style. There is a definite intention to avoid intricate details discernible in the work of many artists.

There appears to be a reason behind this conservative approach. The most important being that this job was neither commissioned by aristocracy nor by the rulers. The main objective of the artist was to sell it to common people as these manuscripts were used for recitations during the rituals or daily prayers in the households. The intention of the artist was not to create a great piece of art but to represent the iconic images of gods or scenes from sacred texts in simple style with summary details. Even the floral borders were also done in a summary way.

The distinct Kashmiri art produced from the seventeenth to the nineteenth century had a fusion of Pahari, Buddhist, Persian, Afghan and Mughal styles. But since these paintings are spread over many places and housed in various museums and archives or with individuals, it is not an easy task to see them all and comment on their evolution.

Kashmiri paintings done during ancient and medieval periods are laden with Gandhara, Gupta and Buddhist Influences. These are in tandem with the sculptures of the period. In the sculptures and paintings of the period, women are shown fleshy with sharp features. Their body parts like legs and breasts are exposed. Their eyes are almond shaped with arched eyebrows.

They wear jewellery. They have long and lovely hair. They have thick lips and plump cheeks. There is an explicit fervour to trace body contours. This appears to be the result of the strict implementation of the *Chitrasutra* guidelines. This is in contrast to what we see later in Kashmir paintings, done between the seventeenth to the early twentieth century.

Examples of Kashmir wall-paintings belonging to the Mughal period are still extant in the Baradaris (summer houses) of the famous Nishat and Shalimar gardens.

In Kashmir, the tradition of temple painting did not die totally after the fourteenth century, Kashmir's art form remained alive in other ways. In the twentieth century also, one saw frescos or paintings in temples. I have seen it in the Ramji temple (Ali Kadal), Shiva temple (Rainawari), Sri Ramchanderji temple (Barbar Shah), Baba Dharam Dass temple, Pratapeshwar temple, Ram Kaul temple (Hari Parbat) and many more temples that were built in the nineteenth or early twentieth centuries during the Dogra rule.

Even if Kashmir School of Art did not survive after the 14th century, it remained alive through other means. Painting and art became a part of the rituals in Kashmiri Pandit families. A painting had to be given to the Yajmaan (patron) by the Kul Purohita (family priest) on Gauri Tritya day. On Gauri Tritya day, every boy and girl in a Kashmiri Brahmin family used to receive from the family priest bright-coloured paintings of the gods and goddesses. Gauri Tritiya was celebrated on the third day of Maaga Shukla Paksh as per the Hindu

Bikrami calendar. The day before Gauri Tritiya was known as Rang Doi. Rang Doi day was dedicated by Kashmiri Pandits for making colourful images of elephants, peacocks, trees, swans and goddess Saraswati on white paper.

Similarly, during the marriages and *Mekhala* (sacred thread) ceremonies, the doors and windows were and are still painted bright with floral designs and the drawings are known as *Krool*.[3] Drawing colourful *Vyoog*[4] or Rangoli in the courtyards during marriages is a very old tradition among Kashmiri Pandits. The *Vyoog* or Rangoli is always drawn over a basic cosmic circle.

Miniature paintings done in Kashmir after the Mughal rule are an inimitable blend of various styles. These carry the old tradition of the Buddhist period while absorbing the Persian and Pahari influences. Kashmir's religious miniature paintings have a long and rich tradition of illustrated/illuminated manuscripts. Many unknown painters have drawn illustrations and illuminated religious texts including the Bhagwat Gita and Bhagwat Purana with paintings showing scenes from the life of Sri Krishna.

From Mughal time, apart from the human body, floral designs, animals, birds, flora and fauna, landscapes, etc. started appearing in the paintings of Kashmir. This could be the influence of the Mughal style that originated from the Safavid tradition of art. However, in miniature art, Safavid artists did not neglect the human body.

Unfortunately, this rich treasure of Kashmiri Miniature Paintings could neither be preserved carefully, nor did it attract the attention of art historians and critics. At the official level in the State of J&K,

3 Krool is an artistic decoration of the main entrance or door of a house with colours. This is done before the start of the actual marriage ceremony. Generally, flowers, leaves, and branches are drawn in bright colours to give an auspicious aura at the entrance. It is also believed that' Krool is drawn for the blissful married life of the couple.

4 Vyoog finds mention in the Nilamata Purana of Kashmir. This practice was known as Bhoomi-Shobha in ancient Kashmir. Dwar-Shobha (Krool in Kashmiri) and Bhoomi-Shobha (Vyoog in Kashmiri) find mention in many ancient texts of the Hindus.

there was and is no initiative for any research in this area, leave alone serious efforts for its revival.

Some useful work has been done by the Indira Gandhi National Centre for Arts, New Delhi by capturing 343 Kashmir paintings in a reprographic form (slides) and creating a digital record thereof. These slides were created from the collections held by the J&K Academy of Art, Culture, and Languages, the Kashmir University (Centre for Central Asian Studies), J&K State Archives, and the SPS Museum, Srinagar. These paintings mostly relate to the period between the eighteenth and nineteenth centuries.

PAHARI MINIATURE ART AND KASHMIR

Noted art historian M S Randhawa writes:

> Proselytism of Islam was at its height during the last years of the reign of Aurangzeb. In the last quarter of the 17th century and first quarter of the 18th century, many Kashmiri Brahmins migrated from Kashmir to the Kangra valley to seek sanctuary in the courts of the Rajas of the Kangra Hill States. It is very likely that Pandit Sieu was one of them.

Pandit Shiv Raina (who later came to be known as Sieu Raina) was well versed in the Pala and Mughal style of art. He sought refuge in the court of Raja Dalip Singh (1695 -1741 AD) of Guler. Nainsukh (Nana) and Manaku (Mana) were his sons who later on revolutionised the Pahari Miniature Art by joining Guler, Basholi, Jasrota and various hilly kingdoms of the western Himalayas.

Was Pandit Sieu (Shiv) Raina working in some Mughal court, or did he come from Kashmir directly? This is a baffling question. But certainly, Shiv Raina came to Guler not knowing that his sons and their progeny would shape the history of Pahari Miniature Art in the hills of what is now known as Himachal Pradesh. Others from this Raina-Razdan clan, who worked as court painters in various kingdoms of the western Himalayas, include Atra, Nikka, Ranjha (Ram

Dayal), Chajju, Harku, Saudagar, Kama, Godhu, Chetu, Khushala, Kiru, Gurusahai, and Fattu. These artists of Kashmiri Pandit ancestry contributed greatly towards the development of the Pahari School of Miniature Art. This group of migrant Brahmins from Kashmir did not move towards the plains of the country probably because of the death and destruction created by the invasions of Nadir Shah and Ahmed Shah Abdali. They remained confined to the hilly kingdoms of the present-day Himachal Pradesh.

Noted artist P N Kachru writes:

> Six generations of Pandit Seu Raina produced about forty-six children, and all of them were artists who penetrated their genius very deep into the milieu of all Himachal principalities, thus embedding the whole treasure-accumulation of four thousand years into their new home of outer Himalayas. It needs yet another treatise to keep their track in all the courts and cultural centres of the region. Nain Sukh is the most prominent and influential painter from this Raina clan.

KASHMIRI ARTISTS IN PUNJAB

In the 19th and early 20th century, many unknown artists and scribes from Kashmir were active in Punjab. They came to Punjab during the harsh winters or were permanent residents in various cities like Amritsar, Lahore, Gujranwala, Sialkot. They earned their livelihood by copying or illuminating and illustrating the religious manuscripts or drawing pictures. This is also confirmed by Karuna Goswamy in her book, *Kashmiri Paintings*. Many paintings and illuminated and illustrated manuscripts done by these unknown artists in Kashmiri style are on display in various museums the world over. Many can be seen in the various museums in the country.

In the 19th century, Pandit Hardas Koul Tota, Pandit Daya Ram Koul Tota, and Pandit Raja Ram Koul Tota (also known as Hardas Tota Naqqash, Daya Ram Tota Naqqash, and Raja Ram Tota Naqqash) and some more persons from this illustrious Koul Tota family were famous painters, calligraphers and artists from Kashmir settled in Lahore. Their paintings and illuminated, illustrated manuscripts are on display in some museums of the world apart from being in possession of some private collectors. The Totas knew Persian. Raja Ram Koul Tota wrote and illuminated the Persian manuscript of *Rajtarangini* which is on display in the National Library of Iran in Tehran. *Ragamala* is another manuscript illuminated by Raja Ram Koul Tota.

In his book, Punjab Paintings, R P Srivastava writes:

> Raja Ram Koul Tota was a calligraphist with Kohinoor Press, Lahore. He was a very good artist. He wrote *Zaffarnama* of Guru Gobind Singh. All the illustrations and paintings in this book have been done by him. Another work by him is *Gulgashat-e-Punjab* written in 1864 CE. It is the history of Punjab from earlier times till the annexation of Punjab in 1849. Then again *Gulabnama* and *Gulzar-e-Kashmir* written by Diwan Kirpa Ram were transcribed by him. Manuscript of *Maha Shiv Puran* was prepared in Samvat 1929 by Daya Ram Koul Tota, father of Raja Ram Koul Tota under the patronage of the Lahore kingdom.

Sham Lal Khaar, the miniature artist from Mattan (Kashmir) says:

> About 100 years ago, many Brahmins from Mattan visited Punjab regularly during the winter season. They would prepare horoscopes, copy religious manuscripts or draw pictures of gods and goddesses for their Yejmaans (patrons) or customers. They visited rural and urban areas of Punjab. They also visited fairs for this work. They were called Katibs and Mussavirs in Punjab. Some people called them Pandulipikaars. Some of them knew Sharda, Sanskrit, Gurmukhi, and drawing. Some persons were also skilled in the art of illuminating religious texts.

ART ON MAPS

Kashmiri artists and artisans have created some spectacular maps either on shawls or on paper. This work has also been reckoned as a part of the tradition known as the 'Kashmir School of Art'. The Map Shawls, created by Kashmiri artists and artisans on Pashmina cloth, are housed in museums like the Victoria and Albert Museum (London), Jaipur Museum (Jaipur, Rajasthan) and Sri Partap Singh Museum (Srinagar). One Kashmiri Map shawl is on display in a museum in Australia while one is held by a private collector. The masterpiece Srinagar City of this work rests in the Victoria and Albert Museum, London. It is reported that this rectangular Pashmina shawl was completed in thirty years. Done with woollen threads, this shawl depicts an embroidered map of entire Srinagar city showing the Dal Lake, the bridges over Jhelum River, Shankracharya Temple, Hari Parbat Fort, Shah-e-Hamdan Mosque, and many other prominent landmarks.

The artistic maps of Sahib Ram Koul also fall in this category. Done with pen and ink and gouache on paper, these artistic maps represent a style prevalent in Kashmir at that point in time. These maps are held in a book called Tirathasangrah (showing sacred springs and pilgrimage centres of Kashmir). These maps have identifying inscriptions in Urdu (Nasta'liq script) and Sanskrit (Nagari script). The Map Shawls and the Tirathsangrah (maps of sacred springs of Kashmir) prepared by Sahib Ram Koul were a part of commissioned work done during the Dogra rule in Kashmir.

WHAT HAPPENED TO KASHMIR'S ART AND SCULPTURE?

Art was subjected to plunder and loot in India for many centuries. Even under stringent laws, the criminals operating in this area managed to ship or airlift this precious wealth from the country. In Kashmir, the extent of plunder and loot of ancient artefacts, paintings and sculptures of the Buddhist and the Hindu periods is colossal. It has happened too often. It is a result of the indifference and apathy from all quarters. The civil society, establishment, and public, in general, have remained unconcerned about the gradual removal of the treasures followed by widespread plunder during the armed militancy of the 1990s. One needs to visit various museums of the world, apart from thousands of individuals who possess these precious treasures to understand the magnitude of the loss of artistic heritage in Kashmir.

Many historians also believe that a large number of artists and craftsmen of Kashmir perished during the invasion of Zulchu (1323 AD) a Tartar chief. Life in Kashmir valley started from scratch after the destruction, killings, and plunder of Zulchu. Zulchu's plunder must have destroyed the works of art and starved artists to death.

The fourteenth century Kashmir witnessed the suppression of the Hindus and large scale demolition of their places of worship. This demolition and destruction were again carried out by other rulers and their allies in the 15th century. Many beautiful sculptures and idols lying in these temples were broken. The details of these demolitions are given in many historical texts and also in some Persian chronicles like Baharistan i Shahi, Tohfatu'l Ahbab, Vaqaat i Kashmir, Twaarikh i Kashmir, etc. All these Persian chronicles have been translated into English by various scholars. Some magnificent temples in Kashmir were razed to the ground and destroyed completely. The present status of some major archaeological sites in Kashmir valley bears ample testimony to these large scale demolitions. Further, the folklore among Kashmiri Pandits speaks of the time when a medieval Sultan of Kashmir created the embankment of Dal Lake by consigning their religious texts and literature into the waters of the lake.

The UNMESH published by Nityanand Shastri Kashmir Research Institute, New Delhi, in its January 1998 issue writes:-

> These prized items like old manuscripts and miniature paintings belong to the fleeing Pandits who left them behind when they had to run for life. The more clever and sophisticated among the looters knew that these treasure troves could well fetch them a fortune and so they set out foraging for them from one deserted house to another. Finding a new avenue of making easy money, several of them collected old manuscripts by the kilogram. Some of them must have indeed hit the jackpot! And so while Kashmir

is burning, the plunderers are earning. Thus it is that several shady business houses have cropped up in the past seven or eight years in and around Srinagar. Some of them are acting as fake research centres, as for example the one that has come up near Nishat, with looted manuscripts neatly stacked for sale. These 'centres' are doing brisk business, striking deals with collectors, antique dealers and societies. It is here that the peddlers and scrap-dealers from Amritsar are proving of great help. But why take the trouble of a longish trip to Amritsar Khaat Bazaar? You could easily bump into a dealer in alleys and lanes of Delhi itself. Their visits from the doomed valley to the country's capital in search of channels of collectors, agents of antique houses and organizations, and to make lucrative bargains of the looted possessions are getting more and more frequent. Often these people put on a mask of sophistication while on the prowl, well-versed in the art of entrapping potential buyers as they are. Their suave behaviour makes many fall to their bait and loosen their purse strings to acquire an old manuscript or a miniature. In a recent case, a birch-bark manuscript in Sharda carrying two miniature paintings was offered by one such dealer to an arts centre for a whopping rupees one lakh.

No systematic study of the 'Kashmir School of Art' has been attempted so far and no one has ventured to prepare an album of these miniatures, notwithstanding their importance in the overall context of the history of Indian art, the Kangra and Pahari styles being but offshoots of this precious school. While a large number of such paintings have been lost - sold by their unscrupulous owners or others to foreigners and private art collectors in the country in a most callous manner, the Institute has managed to acquire about two dozen Kashmiri miniature paintings and NSKRI is in the process of acquiring more.

European visitors started coming to Kashmir from the 19th century.

Not a single visitor went empty-handed. Some manuscripts, some pieces of art or some sculptures were either gifted to them or were freely carried by them because nothing like preservation or protection of this vital heritage existed in the Kashmir valley. Individuals from the west kept visiting Kashmir regularly and searching for the old manuscripts and paintings.

The SPS Museum in Srinagar was also burgled many times (1917, 1937, 1973, 1989 and 2003) and some invaluable artefacts were stolen. In 1995, security forces during a raid on a suspected militant hideout at Chandpora (Shalimar), recovered 35 antique objects relating to the period between 8th to 10th century AD. These were shifted to New Delhi and handed over to the National Museum.

In 2008, I saw some persons in Hazuri Bagh (near Naaz cinema), Khanyar, Baba Demb and some more markets in Srinagar city selling brass/bronze thaalis (food Plates), brass degchaas (big cooking pots), brass samovars (tea kettles), bronze khasus (tea cups), brass hookahs, religious texts in Sharda and Sanskrit and many other items looted from the abandoned houses of the Kashmiri Pandits. I also saw old latticed wooden windows and carved doors of the Pandit houses on sale at Baba Demb Kabaadi market. The looted brass and bronze items were also sold to some metal scrap dealers of Punjab. It was learned that illuminated/illustrated manuscripts in Sharda or Sanskrit and many old paintings were also for sale. I also learned that a large collection of old manuscripts and paintings were with many individuals living at Nishat or in the Dal Lake localities who were engaged in selling them to the European or Indian art dealers/smugglers.

In the turmoil and terrorism of the 1990s, many senior artists from Kashmir lost every single painting lying in their houses or studios after they had to leave the valley in a hurry to save their lives. These paintings were stolen while the houses or studios were put on fire. The list could be endless. These sufferers include Triloke Kaul, Mohan Raina and P N Kachru. Veteran artist Triloke Kaul told me that he lost entire stock of his paintings as also the paintings gifted to him by

valley. They paid these visits up to the end of the nineteenth century. Notable among them were James Duffield Harding, William Carpenter, William Simpson, Capt Molyneux, Mary Popham Blyth and Florence Parbury. These artists drew portraits and landscapes. Most of these European artists were either personal guests of the Maharaja or travellers who passed through Kashmir on their way to Central Asia, Tibet, Gilgit or other places in the inner Himalayas. They hardly interacted with any local artist.

Apart from the European artists, Baba Bishen Singh (1836-1900), a Sikh artist from Amritsar, also visited Kashmir during the second half of the nineteenth century. He painted about 15 watercolours depicting scenes from the social life in Kashmir.

During Maharaja Pratap Singh's rule, the opening of Sir Amar Singh Technical Institute in Srinagar was a landmark step for the revival of the artistic traditions of Kashmir. This institute played a key role in exposing locals to modern artistic trends and styles. The newly-opened institute was affiliated to The City and Guilds Institute, London. A diploma in fine arts was awarded by this Institute to the students. Aurel Stein recommended to the Maharaja the name of Fredrick H Andrews as the first principal of the proposed institute. Frederick Andrews had been the vice-principal of the Mayo School of Art, Lahore. Accordingly, Fredrick Andrews became the first principal of this institute. He left India in 1923. He was followed by J C Mukerjee, another able and brilliant man in the field of fine arts.

Mukerjee was a well-known artists of the Bengal School. It was through him that local artists became familiar with the Bengal School. Shiv Nath Raina, Sansar Chand Baru, Keshav Malik, P N Kachru, Sat Lal Kampasi, J N Mattoo, J N Sapru, Mohan Raina, D N Walli, Som Nath Khosa, Manohar Kaul, Kashi Nath Bhan, Nila Kanth Zadoo, Kailash Nath Fotedar, Amar Nath Vaishnavi, Mohi-ud-Din, Ghulam Rasool, Som Nath Munshi, Shamboo Nath Bhan, Radha Krishen Raina and Mehraj-ud-Din were some notable students of this institute. In June 1942, Sir Amar Singh Technical Institute was converted into the Amar Singh College.

The well-known artist A R Chugtai (1897-1975) is reported to have visited Kashmir twice before the partition of the country. I am not sure how many paintings and etchings he has done with Kashmir as the theme, but I have seen two of his works titled, 'Two Kashmiri Women with Apples' (a watercolour) and 'Kashmiri Woodcutter' (pencil etching on paper) done before 1947. These two works speak about his immense understanding of the natural beauty and widespread poverty in Kashmir during those days.

The famous artist N S Bendre (1910-1992) also lived in Kashmir for three years (from 1936 to 1939) during the rule of Maharaja Hari Singh. He drew many Kashmir landscapes during his stay in Kashmir.

Syed Haider Raza's visit to Kashmir in 1948 culminated in the formation of a branch of the Progressive Artists Association that had been set up in Mumbai in 1947 and had M F Husain, S K Bakre, F N Souza, H A Gade and many more artists as its members. Raza's visit acted as a catalytic agent. He did pioneering work by training some young artists from Kashmir in modern trends of art. Supported by Raza and Percy Brown, three young Kashmiri artists, S N Butt, Triloke Kaul, and P N Kachru formed 'The Progressive Artists Association'. In May 1949, this association held its first art exhibition in Srinagar, which Raza attended. In October 1949, this association held a major art exhibition outside the State. Held in New Delhi, the October 1949 exhibition was inaugurated by Humayun Kabir.

The role of Percy Brown is no less in bringing modern art to Kashmir. He had done a highly commendable work as curator of the Lahore Museum and as principal of the Mayo College of Art, Lahore (1899-1909). Later, he joined as principal of the Government College of Arts and Crafts, Kolkata. After his retirement, Percy Brown along with his wife, settled in Kashmir. Percy Brown's presence in Kashmir proved immensely helpful to the local artists like Triloke Kaul, P N Kachru, S N Butt and D N Walli. In Kashmir, he remained in touch with some known artists and painters who often visited him to seek his guidance. Percy Brown died in 1955 and lies buried in the

Sheikh Bagh cemetery, Amirakadal, Srinagar.

Apart from Percy Brown, well-known artists and art historians like Herman Goetz, H A Gade and Mulk Raj Anand also visited Kashmir and stayed there for some period. They were a source of motivation for local artists.

The Baroda Group: In 1951, Ratan Parimoo was the first person from Kashmir to go to Baroda where he completed his graduation and post-graduation in art. In 1959, he joined the M S University, Baroda as a faculty member and rose to become the head of the Department of Art History and Aesthetics. He is married to the noted artist, Naina Dalal.

Ratan Parimoo was followed by Triloke Kaul. Triloke Kaul is considered as a pioneer and doyen of Modern Art in the J&K State. Triloke Kaul was followed by G R Santosh and Kishori Kaul. Later, Gayoor Hassan, V R Khajuria, Manzoor Rather, Subash Chander Razdan, Shuban Kaw, Bhushen Kaul, Zahoor Zargar, Kuldeep Kaul, Veer Munshi, A R John, Kishenji Kaw, Nasreen Mohsin, Sunil Veshin, Preeti Veshin, Bishember Mehta and many more went to Baroda to learn the art.

After 1947, the art scenario in the State changed for the better. The establishment of the J&K Academy of Art, Culture and Languages in 1958, followed by the opening of the Institute of Music And Fine Arts gave enough impetus to art in the State. Regular art camps held in Kashmir proved of immense help to the local artists. Stalwarts like M F Husain, Lakshman Pai, Biren De, Shanti Dave, Tyeb Mehta, K K Hebber, Jatin Das, V S Gaitonde, Bal Chhabra, Bimal Dasgupta, Ram Kumar, Homi Patel, J Swaminathan, Ratan Parimoo, G M Sheikh, Kashmiri Khosa, Manu Parikh, Kishori Kaul, Shamshad Hussain, B C Sanyal, G R Santosh and many more attended these camps. The J&K Academy of Art, Culture, and Languages also started acquiring works of the artists.

The J&K Academy of Art, Culture and Languages has a large collection of old miniature paintings from Jammu and Kashmir. The details of 83 miniature paintings are uploaded in the website of the

J&K Academy of Art, Culture and Languages under 'Kashmir Miniature' collection. Apart from this, there are 65 pencil sketches and miniature paintings uploaded as the 'Jammu Miniature' collection.

It also procured paintings of Modern artists from Kashmir. Today, the actual physical status of these 148 precious miniature paintings is not known, especially after the devastating floods of September 2014.

The School of Design was started in Kashmir in the late fifties to develop designs for traditional handicrafts. New designs were created at this school apart from the reorientation of old designs. The School of Design created thousands of new designs, thereby building a treasure house of designs or a Craft Museum. The progressive trio, Triloke Kaul, S N Butt and P N Kachru were employed in this school. Later Suraj Tiku, A K Raina and some more artists joined the School of Design.

In the 1950s, the government opened the Institute of Music and Fine Arts in Jammu and Srinagar. The two wings of the institute have an independent department of painting and sculpture.

As a result of these broad-based initiatives after 1950, we have many talented persons in the field of painting and sculpture in Jammu as well as in Kashmir. Some artists from J&K, who made a mark on the State, national or international art scene are, Sansar Chand Baru, G R Santosh, Mohan Raina, Santokh Singh, Bansi Parimu, Kishori Kaul, Bhushen Kaul, Vijay Gupta, Chandu Lal Dogra, Vidya Rattan Khajuria, Dwarika Nath Gigoo Rajkamal, Manohar Kaul, Masood Hussain, Veer Munshi, Rajindra Tiku (sculpture), Maharaj Bhat, Pran Kishore Kaul, Shuban Krishen Kaw, N D Jamwal, Vijay Saraf, A R John, Mohammad Sadiq, M A Mehboob, Nasreen Mohsin, Gokul Dembi, Shabir Santosh, Kamal Nain Bhan, Zahoor Zargar, T S Batra, Shuja Sultan, Sant ji Sultan, B K Sultan (sculpture), A K Raina, Fida Hussain, Umesh Kaul, Kapil Kaul, Usha Nehru, P K Razdan, Rohit Verma, Arshad Sualeh, Farhat Khan, Tariq Saif Ali, Vijay Kaul, Rajendra Patwari, Fauzia Snober Qazi, Mir Imtiaz (sculpture), Shabir Mirza (sculpture), Ravinder Jamwal (sculpture), Panchsheel Kaul, Bashir Shora, Gobind Kaur (sculpture), Nasreen Shahzadi, Ashok Mehra,

Shaika Muhi (sculpture), K K Gandhi, Vinay Khajuria, Ashutosh Sapru, Suman Gupta, Bhushan Kesar, Anuradha Rishi, Naushad H Gayoor, O P Sharma, Kirtan Dev Sharma, Jang S Verman, Bhuvnesh Raina, Sajood Sailani, Vinay Khajuria, Shafi Chaman, Inder Salim, Iftikhar Jaffar, Raj Kumar Sharma, Bishember Mehta (sculpture), Ganesh Sharma (sculptor), Vijay Zutshi (sculpture), Deeba Amin, Shama Sondhi, Sohan Singh Billawaria (Basholi miniature), Aslam Naqshbandi, Neeraj Raina, Rajan Wattal, Harshvardan Sharma, Lovesh Sharma, Suneeta Handoo, Ravi Dhar, Tsering Wangdu (Thangka painter), Nawang Tsering (sculptor), Dorji Dadul (wood carving), Chimet Rigzin (sculptor), Tsering Gurmat (sculptor), M Y Bacha, Showkat Kathijoo, Milan Sharma, Geeta Das, Mir Niyaz, Mohammad Iqbal (sculpture), M Akram Khan, Mohammad Irfan Bhat, Jagpal Singh (sculpture), Rohit Verma, Santosh Tikoo, Hima Kaul (sculpture), Chander Parkash (sculpture), Tariq Mehmood Saifi, Chushool Mahaldar, Nabeel Sultan, Kanue Amin, Mamoon Ahmed, Zoya Khan, Syed Mujtaba Rizvi, Vikas Khajuria, Vikas Dogra (sculpture), Anil Nakhasi, Rukaya Wani, Sukhjeet Kukkal (sculpture), Surpal Singh Slathia, Devi Dass Khattri (sculpture), Amit Singh Slathia, Brij Pal Anand (sculpture), Veerji Sumbli, Mahvash Masood, Javid Iqbal, Shafia Shafi, Onaiza Drabu, Waseem Mushtaq, Altaf Khan and many others.

Raqib Shaw is a UK-based artist from Kashmir. He paints with enamels, using a needle-sharp porcupine quill. Breathtaking in their intricacy, complexity and flamboyant colours, his paintings are the product of months of intense work. His bronze sculptures have created a buzz in the world of art. Some years ago, Shaw's Garden of Earthly Delights III, sold for a record price of $5.49 million. With that price, he has price-wise surpassed many senior Indian artists including S H Raza.

TERRORISM AND EXILE

In 1989 when Kashmir started witnessing stray bomb blasts or cross firing incidents, many people felt puzzled. Kashmiri society had never seen such things. Initially, it was very difficult for Kashmiris to believe that such incidents could be the result of a well-planned armed insurgency aided and abetted by the enemy across the border. The general comments that cropped up at such incidents were:

> It is a ploy used by the Central government. Possibly they want to topple the elected government.
>
> To gain political mileage, some people are doing these blasts and firing. It is just a temporary phenomenon.
>
> What can happen over here with all-around army's presence? We are all safe here.
>
> These blasts are not directed towards Pandit minority. No need to panic.

National Conference activist, Mohammad Yusuf Halwai was gunned down in August 1989 for he dared to leave his lights on during the Independence Day in August 1989, when JKLF had called for a total blackout. And by September 1989, indications pointed towards the presence of Pakistan-trained and highly motivated young boys with automatic guns and other deadly ammunition in their hands. These highly motivated boys had instructions from their handlers to wipe away all sympathisers of India or Indian presence in the Valley. Emerging from the narrow lanes and alleys of Srinagar city, this militancy quickly engulfed the entire Kashmir valley, the way fog engulfs visibility to create darkness. Noted poet Dina Nath Nadim, in his Kashmiri poem 'Vunal' or 'Fog' writes:

FOG

We never saw its face,
never did we see its back either,
shapeless,
like a long-forgotten thought,
or an unfamiliar reflection that turned cold.
Someone puts up a question,
What is your Name?
Are you Fog?
Very silently it moved past the river banks

and filled the lanes and narrow paths.

Measuring passageways
and looking carefully at everything around,
it swept us,
like the sorrows of this existence
that are delivered from all sides by both the hands.
Engulfing everything,
It made everyone slip into obscurity,
surely, it shall vanish of its own,
die with warmth
and melt away.
At that moment alone,
we may be able to see each other's face.

After Neel Kanth Ganju (retired judge killed on 4 November 1989), Tika Lal Taplu (BJP leader killed on 13 September 1989), Prem Nath Bhat (senior advocate killed on 27 December 1989) and some more killings in the second half of the year 1989, panic, fear and gloom had set in the minds of the minuscule Kashmiri Pandit community. Noted Persian scholar and historian, Kashi Nath Pandita recounts, 'In September 1989, when Tika Lal Taplu was killed, there was fear and fright on all faces. Through a widely circulated English newspaper, I addressed a letter to Azadi movement leaders to clear their stand towards Kashmir Pandits and other minorities. The reply received by me closed all options. We were told to join the Azadi movement or leave Kashmir. No other option was put forth. The situation at that time was a clear signal to the Hindus and other minorities living in the Valley'.

Allama Iqbal has summed up this situation in his poetry as:

Chhupa kar aasteen mein bijliyaan rakhi hain garduun ne
Aanaadil bagh ke gaafil na baithen aashiyaanon mein
Wattan ki fikr kar nadaan museebat aanewaali hai
Teri barbaadiyon ke mashware hain aasmaanon mein

The arched sphere has concealed lightning in its sleeve,
Let not the nightingales of the garden sit carefree in their nests,
Oh, the ignorant! Think of your homeland, the tragedy waits in wings,
Consultations for your destruction are being held in the skies.

From December 1989, things started worsening in the Kashmir valley. Abductions, killing of the innocents, bomb blasts, fear, suspicion and the complete breakdown of law and order created panic in all minds. Many armed militant groups trained and supported by Pakistan started arriving on the scene.

On 4 January 1990, Kashmiri Pandits shrank in fright when the militant organisation, Hizbul Mujahideen, issued a public notice in the widely circulated Urdu newspaper, *Aftab*, threatening all Hindus to leave Kashmir immediately or face consequences. On 14 January 1990, another Srinagar based Urdu newspaper, *Al-Safa*, republished the same warning. Panic gripped the entire Kashmiri Pandit community on the intervening nights of 18th and 19th January, when loudspeakers from the mosques in the entire Kashmir valley blared pro-Azadi slogans, asking people to come out on the roads. That night, the intimidating slogans in the streets asked people to make Kashmir free from all the enemies of the Azadi movement.

Hit lists were pasted on the outer walls of the mosques. These lists had names of many Kashmiri Pandits alleged to be working as informants. This created panic in the minds of the listed persons who had either to leave Kashmir to save their lives or stay and get killed. In this hostile and charged environment, the minuscule Kashmiri Pandit community felt threatened and unsafe. Anybody could be killed and labelled as Mukhbir (Informant) and nobody dared to react. Thus, Kashmir with its age-old traditions of tolerance and brotherhood became a dangerous place to live in.

Fear defined behavioural response of people to any and every incident. Out of fear, Muslims neighbours kept silent when an innocent Pandit was killed by the armed terrorists. Many Kashmiri

Pandit families were advised by their Muslim neighbours to leave Kashmir. They admitted that they had no control over the events and the way things were shaping up. The gun culture changed the social discourse in Kashmir. From tolerance and pluralism, it shifted to exclusiveness and fundamentalism. With no one and no strong governments to fall back upon, the Kashmiri Pandits felt helpless, insecure, and alienated. After a spate of killings was unleashed upon this hapless community, they left Kashmir, taking their bare bodies with them. The plight of the Pandits at that time is aptly described by Ali Sardar Jafri's couplet:

Kaam ab koyi na aayega bas ek dil ke siwa
Raaste bandh hain sab koocha-e-qaatil ke siwa.

No one shall now come to our rescue except our own heart,
For us, other than the assassin's street,
every path lies blocked.

The atmosphere turned into a mass exodus after 19 January 1990. This is how poet Rafiq Raaz describes the tragic migration of Pandits from the Valley:

Patay laraz rahay thhay khatraa thaa aandhiyon kaa
Ghar ho rahay thhay khaali mausam tha hijraton kaa

The leaves kept trembling
and the hurricane was about to unleash itself,
The houses were being emptied
and the season of migration had set in.

A split between Pandits and Muslims had been tactfully engineered by the armed militants. These militant groups succeeded in creating a situation where no person looked beyond hate and prejudice towards the Pandits.

The Kashmiri poem *'Assi von na kinhi'* or 'Not a word did we utter' composed by poet Radhey Nath Masarat (1939-2021) remains one of the most powerful poems representing fear, silence and plight of people who were driven out from their homes and hearths in 1990. In this poem, Masarat is forthright and direct in conveying the helplessness, pain and suffering of the people who were subjected to all sorts torment and agony by armed militants and their cohorts .

Baarav dhyet dazavein naaran von
'Hey Saaf Kariekh'
Akhbaarav von 'Naahaq maariekh'
Assi von na kinhi.....
Gaeli zeiv assi gayi
aess kyaah vanahav
pyatha-kani aess Dhuryodhan Shakuni
Zaareiv gyundh zaar ta aess haariekh
Assi von na kinhi...

The fire that burnt us,
kept complaining and crying:
'Alas! they have been finished and wiped away'
The newspapers carried our story:
'Innocents have been killed'
Yet, not a word did we utter.
We turned dumb,
What could we say otherwise
when Shakuni and Duryodhan became
masters of our destiny?
The dice players played their game
and lost us as their stake.
Yet, not a word did we utter.

There are yet inspiring stories, though few, of some unknown men, who never lost their objectivity or who were never swayed by the prevailing frenzy, hate and negativity of the 1990s in the Kashmir valley. One person amongst such few men is Mohammad Amin, the proprietor of the National Masala/Kanwal Spices, Anantnag, Kashmir. Mohammad Amin paid salary to Prem Nath Kaul, his employee from village Nanil, regularly till death (for more than 11 years) after May 1990. In May 1990, Prem Nath was pulled out from a Matador (public transport vehicle) by armed boys near Krungsoo village when he was returning from his work. He was threatened with dire consequences if he was again seen in Anantnag. Branding him an informant, he was asked to leave Kashmir. Prem Nath never worked at Mohammad Amin's factory after the May 1990 incident: initially out of fear and later due to poor health. Prem Nath Kaul and his wife stayed in Kashmir after 1990, solely on Mohammad Amin's support. Prem Nath refused to leave Kashmir when his son left the Valley in 1990 due to threats and fear. A religious man, Prem Nath wrote and sang Leelas in Kashmiri. He played on harmonium and banjo. To this aged couple, Mohammad Amin did what a son is supposed to do for his aged and dependent parents. I am sure there must be many more unknown men like Mohammad Amin. Prem Nath's son, Moti Lal Kaul recounts:

> Beyond what you already know, I need to make some addition. My father was a spiritual man. He never left Kashmir due to some unbelievable attachment. He advised me to leave, when I received some threats but totally refused to move out in 1990 even under grave threats and warnings. He wrote poetry and sang Naats and Leelas. Apart from paying regular salary to my father for no work after May 1990, Mohammad Amin paid pension to my mother for about 15 years after the death of my father. My father died in 2001. Mohammad Amin would also visit my parents regularly to see that they are fine. Mohammad Amin is a rare human being. In 1990, he was like an island of hope and goodwill in an ocean of hate, darkness, threats and intimidation for my parents.

The armed militancy brought days of darkness and gloom. It brought innumerable hardships, pain, and suffering for common masses. Fear, death, destruction, and darkness defined Kashmir after 1990.

Many young boys were sucked into this armed militancy resulting in lifelong pain to their parents. Smiles on the faces of many mothers were replaced by tears and sighs. Every day, one saw local newspapers full of resignations by mainstream political workers to save their lives. Posters that contained threatening messages to all the Kashmiris, were pasted on the walls throughout the Valley. People were directed to follow the Islamic rules which included abidance by the strict Islamic dress code, total prohibition on alcohol and closure of cinemas and video parlours. Fear ruled and silenced all liberal voices. Fear made people submit to the diktats of the armed militants who directed them to wipe out the word INDIA from all the commercial signboards that were painted green. People were asked to reset their watches to the Pakistan Standard Time.

During this period, a systematic propaganda war was unleashed by radio from across the border through a powerful and highly upgraded transmission system. Songs like *'Aey Chinaron ki vaadi ke sarv e ravaan tez chal'* meaning 'O, cypress from the valley of Chinar trees, move fast' and many more similar songs broadcast regularly were simply meant to incite youth in Kashmir valley to armed revolt. These POK radio stations were clearly heard right up to Kulgam and Shopian areas of south Kashmir .

The armed militants made people believe that Azadi was at hand. Frantic inquiries were made by many persons from the bankers as to what would happen to the currency notes held by them in their homes. A desperate lookout for the US dollars had started in a hush-hush way. The schools, colleges, banks, offices and other establishments remained mostly closed. Public transport was off the roads. Silence, suspicion and insecurity crept into the behaviour of people. The gun-wielding militants drove many people towards developing the Stockholm Syndrome. Terms like Azadi, Nizam-e-Mustafa,jihad,

Kafir, Mukhbir, and Mujahid gained currency.

Theatre and art-related activities vanished from the landscape. Smoke, firing, fire, killings, crackdowns, curfew, abandoned houses, deserted roads and terror made life hell for those who opted to stay back in Kashmir. Many Muslim families also moved out of the Valley for many reasons, viz. their pro-India attitude, their love for peace and human dignity and the education of their children. The armed militants imposed a ban on free speech. The situation of that time is rightly described by the noted Kashmiri poet, Farooq Nazki in his Poem 'Naad Laayey' or 'I shall call you back'. This poem is included in his Sahitya Akademi award-winning Kashmiri poetry collection, 'Naar Hyotun Kazalwanus' or 'Kazalwan is on fire'. Kazalvan is a beautiful forest range near Bandipora in Kashmir. The poem reads:

> Fear dangled from doors and windows,
> while the masked devil kept waiting in the courtyard.
> The cat kept mewing in its burrow dug in the Chinar tree trunk,
> stammering for words,
> how could we cry?
>
> The youthful Iris flower fell to dust,
> tulips grew wild on mud roofed houses,
> and frighteningly blew the wind like a hungry lion
> that comes down to the village in mid-January
> from the forest after the winter snowfall,
> and goes wild after every prey.

In his Interview to journalist Omkar Razdan, Sufi Ghulam Mohammad, editor of the popular Urdu newspaper, *The Srinagar Times*, describes the condition that prevailed in January 1990:

> Question: As per a survey by *Kashmir Images*, a weekly published in Kashmir, 68 per cent Muslims believe that Pandits betrayed them in their hour of distress. Do you agree?
>
> Sufi: No, I am not in agreement at all. The Kashmiri Pandits were

not in a position to help in any way. They were compelled to leave their homes, their jobs, and their land overnight. So, what is this betrayal all about?

Q: The reference obviously is to the suffering of common Muslims in the street during cordon-cum-search operations, crackdowns and arbitrary arrests resorted to by the security forces to control the militancy. Have they not been wronged?

Sufi: Majority community should understand that they are the victims of a proxy war. This war was neither engineered nor supported by Pandits. In fact, they were the first victims of the scheme which forced them to leave the State. Therefore, this is an unfair 'charge' against Pandits.

Q: The political chief of Jamaat-i-Islami says that not a single cadre of his 'Jamat' was responsible for Pandit killings. What is your view?

Sufi: (smiles): Technically he may be right. Even today they claim that there is no connection between the present killings and Jamat-i-Islami. But the ground realities should also support their views.

Q: Most people in the Valley blame Mr Jagmohan, the erstwhile Governor of the State, for encouraging the Pandits' flight. Do you agree?

Sufi: It is a total lie. It is a part of systematic propaganda. The Pandit flight from the Valley was the sequel to a plan hatched well in advance from the State. It had nothing to do with Jagmohan.

Q: Why could Mr Jagmohan not organise Pandit camps in the 30-odd military stations in the Valley itself?

Sufi: The situation was too bad for Jagmohan when he assumed office. Mr Rajiv Gandhi (not prime minister then) came for an overnight visit. Both I and Jagmohan were present in the Centaur Hotel on the lake. Rajiv Gandhi said, 'Kashmir is slipping away from us'. Such was the situation for Jagmohan. Even Mr M L Fotedar, and the then Deputy Prime Minister, Mr Devi Lal, were

accompanying Rajiv Gandhi when he said so.
Q:What was the problem in housing the Pandits in makeshift barracks, schools, Dharmshalas, institutional army buildings close to military stations? The whole race of Pandits would have been saved from the tragedy of deserting their homeland?
Sufi: One has to appreciate the January 1990 situation in the Valley. Jagmohan stayed in Jammu for one night. He took a flight from Jammu and arrived in Srinagar Raj Bhavan the next day. He called some of his friends. He called me too. Had I known that the situation was as bad as it later turned out to be, frankly, I would not have gone to Raj Bhavan. There were just three people in the room when I arrived at the Srinagar Raj Bhavan. He offered a cup of tea to me but there was nobody to bring one. I saw him go towards the kitchen three times; presumably, he made the tea himself. There was no administration worth the name anywhere in the State, I mean in the Valley. The police stations all over the Valley were centres of operation for the militants. Jagmohan could not have done anything. Nearly 32,000 Kashmiri Pandit houses have been burnt since 1991. Is there Jagmohan's hand in this too? People like you, even in 1997, need courage to come to the Valley. Otherwise, it is still not safe here. Look what happened in Sangrampura in March 1997, when seven Pandits were mercilessly gunned down.
Q: What is your opinion of the *Kashmir Images* Survey in which 76 per cent of its Muslims population wanted the Kashmiri Pandits back in the Valley?
Sufi: The fact is that even today, your erstwhile neighbours wish that you all should come back. They would even extend warm hospitality to you when you visit them. But even they will be harbouring a sense of fear while dealing with Pandits. We all need to wait for normalcy which is not yet in sight.

This interview appears in the book
The Trauma of Kashmir-The Untold Reality, by Omkar Razdan

The National Conference president, Omar Abdullah, while commenting on the exodus of Kashmiri Pandits from the Valley in 1990, wrote on his official Blog:

> It's so easy to say that we will lay down our lives to bring Kashmiri Pandits back to the Valley and I appreciate the sentiment as I am sure the Kashmiri Pandits reading it will. Pity! this sentiment was missing when our mosques were being used to drive these people out. None of us was willing to stand up and be counted when it mattered. None of us grabbed the mikes (microphones) in the mosques and said, 'This is wrong and the Kashmiri Pandits had every right to continue living in the Valley'. Our educated, well-to-do relatives and neighbours were spewing venom 24 hours a day and we were mute spectators, either mute in the agreement or mute in abject fear but mute, nonetheless.

Till his last day, Bansi Parimu believed the tragedy of 1990 was transient and it would end soon. Even thirty years later, as we remember the artist Parimu, Kashmiri Pandits are still homeless.

BIBLIOGRAPHY

The Kashmiri Pandit by Anand Koul published by Utpal Publications.

Olympia's Progeny, French Impressionist and Post Impressionist Paintings, Wildenstein , New York.

Kalhana's *Rajatarngini,* translated by R S Pandit and published by Sahitya Akademi, New Delhi.

The *Nilamata Purana* (Volume I and II) in English translation by Dr Ved Kumari Ghai, published by The J&K Academy of Art, Culture, and Languages.

'J&K Museum Speaks' published by the Department of Archives, Archeology and Museums, J&K Government.

Kashmir: Painting and Theatre in Kashmir Suraj Tiku's Journey, by Dr Ramesh Tamiri.

Kashmiri Paintings by Karuna Goswamy.

Kashur Qalam' by S Dheer, published by the J&KAACL, Srinagar.

Kashmir Sculptures (volume I and II) by J L Bhan.

Kashi Nath Dhar Rachnavali edited by Prof Chaman Lal Sapru.

The Valley of Kashmir by Walter R Lawrence.

'Approaches to Bharata's Natyashastra' edited by Amrit Srinivasan (Sangeet Natak Akademi).

Thirty Years in Kashmir by Arthur Neve.

The Rajatarangini of Jonaraja translated by J C Dutt.

A Muslim Missionary in Mediaeval Kashmir (Tohfatu'l Ahbab), translated into English by Dr Kashi Nath Pandita.

Miraas (Jan.–June 2019 issue), an English magazine published from New Delhi.

Punjab Painting (Study in Art and Culture) by R P Srivastava.

Hindu Shrines of Kashmir by R L Bhat.

Ancient Monuments of Kashmir by R C Kak.

'Indian Court Paintings - 16th to 19th Century', published by the Metropolitan Museum of Art, New York.

Sheeraza No.5/230 published by the J&K Academy of Art, Culture, and Languages, Dec. 2015-Jan. 2016 issue.

Booklet published by Christie's titled 'Impressionist and Modern Paintings, Drawings and Sculptures (Part I)', for their auction dated 13 November 1996.

A History of Indian painting – Modern Period by Krishna Chaitanya.

The Trauma of Kashmir-The Untold Reality by Omkar Razdan.

Crescent Over Kashmir: Politics of Mullaism by Anil Maheshwari, published by Rupa and Co in 1993.

some prominent artists on the national scene. Sudesh Raina (son of artist Mohan Raina) told me that about 1000 paintings of his father were stolen and some of these have travelled to the US and some European countries. A similar story of total loss was conveyed to me by Umakant Kachru, son of artist P N Kachru.

One is surprised to find that there is nothing significant left on ground of what was a glorious school of painting in Kashmir while inestimable sculptures in stone, metal, terracotta, and wood (created for both the Hindu and the Buddhist faiths) relating to the period from 3rd century AD to 12th century AD are seen in many museums the world over apart from being principally displayed in the SPS Museum, Srinagar. However, it is satisfying to see the efforts put in by most of the museums in Europe and the US for preservation and protection of the prized manuscripts, paintings, sculptures and other artefacts of Kashmir.

REVIVAL OF ARTISTIC TRADITION IN KASHMIR & EXPOSURE TO MODERN ART

Though up to the end of first quarter of the twentieth century, modern trends in paintings created by artists like Van Gogh, Edward Manet, Paul Gauguin, Paul Cézanne, Claude Monet and many more were almost unknown in Kashmir, yet many talented persons from the Valley had the will and desire to look beyond what was happening in the Valley. Some enterprising individuals took the lead in this direction and dared to cross the passes and get some training. In the first and second quarters of the twentieth century, many travelled to Lahore, Gwalior, Kolkata and other cities for learning music and other fine arts. One prominent name in the field of art in that period happens to be of Pandit Maheshwar Nath Dhar (1888-1971) who went to Gwalior in 1910 to learn the skills of painting. Kashmir also had a miniature artist cum sculptor, Narayan Kachru Murtgar, who lived through the latter part of the 19th and early 20th century.

During the Dogra rule, many European artists visited the Kashmir